D1241090

THE STORY OF
AMERICAN ROADS

VAL HART

THE STORY OF AMERICAN ROADS

THE JUNIOR LITERARY GUILD
AND
WILLIAM SLOANE ASSOCIATES, INC.
Publishers   New York

Typography and format designed by
LEONARD W. BLIZARD

PRINTED AT THE COUNTRY LIFE PRESS, GARDEN CITY, N.Y.

FOR MARTHA SCOTT HART

who wanted to know where roads begin and where
they end and how people used to travel over them

PREFACE

Any path, any trail, any road, exists because there is a need for it. The little path leading from a farmhouse down to the spring was worn deep by the feet of thirsty people. Country roads leading from farms to modern highways are needed for hauling farm products into cities. The splendid highways which now connect American cities and towns have been built because of the growing need of people to trade with each other. The more need there is for a road, the better the road will be—and without the modern roads of today the United States could not be the great country it is.

This is the story of American roads—why and how they were built, and where they led. It is also the story of the men who made the roads, and the women and children who journeyed with them. They were courageous people, although they never stopped to think about it. It took courage and patience and strength to cut a path through wilderness country.

ACKNOWLEDGMENTS

The author gratefully acknowledges the help given in preparing the manuscript by the American

Road Builders' Association; Mr. Albert C. Rose, Mr. R. E. Royall, and Mr. Paul Donald of the Bureau of Public Roads; Mr. Richard Tupper and Mr. Michael Frome of the American Automobile Association; and Mr. Walter Belson of the American Trucking Association. Historical societies in the forty-eight states lent invaluable assistance, as did many road-building machinery companies.

All but one of the pictures and photographs in the book are by courtesy of the Bureau of Public Roads, which graciously allowed the selection and reproduction of the excellent material, both historical and modern, from their files. The photograph of Lake Shore Drive is from the Chicago Park District.

"Shoot the Buffalo" and "Sweet Betsy from Pike" are quoted from *A Treasury of American Song,* by Olin Downes and Elie Siegmeister, published by Alfred A. Knopf, Inc., New York, 1943.

The quotation on pages 84 and 85 is from *A History of Travel in America,* by Seymour Dunbar, Copyright 1915, 1943, used by special permission of the publishers, The Bobbs-Merrill Company, Inc.

The "chantey of Erie Canal movers" and the quotation on pages 102 and 103 are from *New York— the Canal State,* by Francis P. Kimball, published by The Argus Press, 1937, and reprinted by permission of the author.

"The Long Road West" is from *Songs of the Trail,* by Henry Herbert Knibbs, published 1920 by Houghton Mifflin Company, and reprinted by their permission.

"Daisy Bell" is reprinted by permission of Francis, Day and Hunter, Ltd.

"Song of the Truck," by Doris Frankel, is reprinted by courtesy of the du Pont Company, sponsors of *Cavalcade of America.*

CONTENTS

CONTENTS

AMERICA ON WHEELS

THE ROAD AHEAD

ILLUSTRATIONS

MAPS BY RAFAEL PALACIOS

THE BEGINNINGS

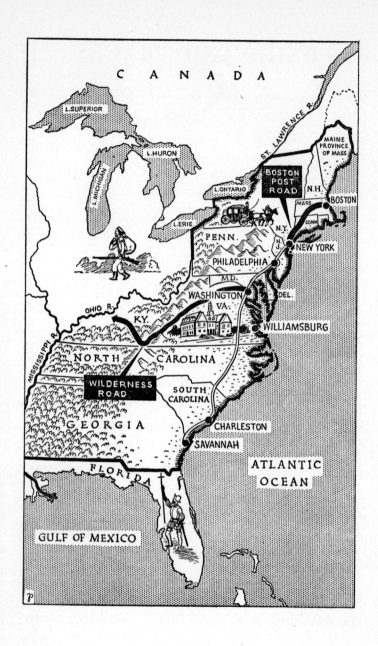

CANADA

L.SUPERIOR

L.HURON

L.MICHIGAN

L.ONTARIO

L.ERIE

ST. LAWRENCE R.

MAINE
PROVINCE
OF MASS

BOSTON
POST
ROAD

N.H.

MASS.

BOSTON

CONN.

N.Y.

NEW YORK

PENN.

N.J.

PHILADELPHIA

MD.

DEL.

OHIO R.

WASHINGTON

VA.

KY.

WILLIAMSBURG

MISSISSIPPI R.

NORTH   CAROLINA

WILDERNESS
ROAD

SOUTH
CAROLINA

GEORGIA

CHARLESTON

SAVANNAH

FLORIDA

ATLANTIC
OCEAN

GULF OF MEXICO

1. TRAILS AND TRACES

> Father, help us
> You are close by in the dark.
> Hear us and help us.
> Take away the white man
> Send back the buffalo
> We are poor and weak
> We can do nothing alone.
> Help us to be as we once were—
> Happy hunters of buffalo.
>
> *Sioux Prayer*

Like life-supplying veins in the broad, rich body of America is its system of three million miles of traversable roads. Some of these are expensive four- and six-lane highways which carry great burdens of commerce and uncountable thousands of motorists on the nation's business and the people's pleasures. Others are smaller roads connecting one town with another town, one city with another. And then there are the narrow dirt roads which seem lost in those out-of-the-way places where America still lives as it did in quieter times.

But they are all American roads, springing from the pathways of our national beginning. Our progress rode along them and will ride, inevitably, down the ones yet to be built. And so they are more than roads; they are the long-winding story of the greatness of America. Let us swing back down them into the past:

Five hundred years ago America was frighteningly and dangerously distant from Europe. It must have seemed to many Europeans as remote as the moon or the planet Mars seem to us today. It was a land of stillness and forest darkness. The only human sounds were those made by Indians as they went about their villages and on their hunting trips.

There were the unceasing sounds of nature, the songs of birds, the rush of the winds, the rustle of small animals in underbrush, and the thunderings of great beasts, the buffalo and moose, over the plains and forest trails. The surf played on the shores, and thunder rolled across the mountains and rivers, and the dark forests. But otherwise it was quiet; and when the sun went down America became a dark and lonely land. Only the moonlight, the flashes of lightning, the gleam of stars and scattered campfires broke the darkness.

There were then two kinds of roads in America, the only types needed. These were the Indian paths and the animal trails made by deer, elk, and buffalo. Sixty million buffalo roamed North America—almost half as many as there are now people in the

United States. They tore out wide roadways over the continent, spreading as far west as the Blue Mountains in Oregon, as far south as the Rio Grande, as far north as the Great Lakes, and southeast to Kentucky. Besides these long highways used in the animals' migrations to better climate, many short paths or "traces" led to salt licks and special feeding and watering places.

The buffalo chose the easiest and most direct route for their trails. Whenever possible they followed the ridges of mountains, for usually the ground on the high slopes was bare of trees and bushes. In summer the rain ran off the high trails and in winter whipping winds blew the snow away. As centuries passed the buffalo trails, wide and hard-packed, became real pathways into the wilderness country.

The Indians of five hundred years ago needed only simple trails for hunting and for war, and like the buffalo they used the easy route along the high ridges. But they had other reasons for liking the mountain paths: From high trails they could make smoke signals, and keep a sharp watch for enemy or game moving through the valley.

The Indian path was narrow, on an average fifteen inches wide. The travelers walked in single file; fearing ambuscade, they were careful to have trees and bushes close on both sides of their paths. Knowing the movements of the sun and stars, the Indians never needed to mark their trails. They could tell the north side of a hill or mountain by many small signs—the bend of the trees, the moss, the way the leaves grew. All marking of trees, or "blazing," was done by white men.

Indian trails lay at random like windblown feathers over the land. They were beaten out in the everyday business of making a living—the trails lay where the Indians hunted for their food. Game often grew scarce near the villages, new hunting grounds were sought, and trails were tramped down in the trek toward better hunting.

When the Indians could reach game country by river, however, they did so; the Iroquois, who at one time owned the country from the Blue Ridge Mountains north to the Great Lakes, traveled by canoe along the "Oyo" (Ohio) River and its northern branches. Within a hunting ground, hunting parties would break up to follow the many little animal paths which crisscrossed through it. The war trails, usually called "Warrior's Paths," were the great routes between enemy Indian nations. They were few in number compared to the many hunting trails, but over the centuries the feet of painted warriors had worn them wide and deep. Along the way were thousands of secret places where the Indians hid, and wide, open areas where they camped.

In the early sixteenth century white missionaries and explorers began to use the buffalo and Indian trails as they pushed farther and farther into the wilderness. So did the fur traders and pioneers, who came later. Their arrival meant calamity to the Indians, for the white men killed buffalo—for food, for hides, or merely for sport. The bones of the great animals were strewn over the plains to bleach in the sun, and in time the vast herds were reduced to only a few hundred.

Long bitter wars drove the red men far from the best hunting grounds, but the Indians remembered their old days, their lost lands. As inexorably they were driven westward before the increasing force of the white men, they looked back with sorrow to the lands they had lost, where their sons were trained to warriorhood, where great names were made in battles, and where their game now roamed to test the skill of other marksmen. They were forced into more uncertain hunting grounds where disputed claims only turned them to interminable wars against each other.

And along with everything else, the white man took over for his own use the roads carved out of the wilderness by the Indians and the buffalo.

2. THE FIRST ROADS

The forest track trodden by the hob-nailed shoes of these sturdy Englishmen has now a distinctness which it never could have acquired from the light tread of a hundred times as many moccasins. . . . And the Indians coming from their distant wigwams to view the white man's settlement marvel at the deep track which he makes, and perhaps are saddened by a flitting presentiment that this heavy tread will find its way all over the land.

Nathaniel Hawthorne

The Spanish, who came to America early in the sixteenth century, sailing up from the West Indies to claim land for the King of Spain, looking for the Northwest Passage, for gold, or to convert the heathen, followed the old Indian trails from Florida to Texas, to New Mexico, and into California. They were the first white men to dare the new wilderness, these conquistadors wearing shining armor and mounted on armored horses. Gradually they carved out an interlocking system of roads over their lands in the new world, calling the network of trails *Los Caminos Reales*. Each individual road was called *El Camino Real*—The Royal Highway.

Developing northward from the capital at Mexico City, the first *camino real* crossed the Rio Grande to El Paso in the early 1500's. Eventually, as missionaries and adventurers pushed through the wilderness, three main branches of *los caminos reales* stemmed from this first trail: one fanning eastward to St. Augustine, Florida; one northward to Santa Fe; and one westward to San Diego.

Ponce de León's unhappy wanderings through Florida during the eight years following his discovery, in 1513, of the peninsula had proved to be the beginning of the eastern section of the Spanish continental network of trails; but more than forty years passed after his death before the Spaniards reached San Antonio, Texas. By 1603 the wilderness trail stretched to Santa Fe, New Mexico, and was reaching out for the Pacific Coast.

The French arrived in Canada under Champlain in 1608 and settled around the St. Lawrence River Valley. La Salle and other explorers, attempting to cut through the wilderness to China, began to dream of a mighty "New France." The Spanish jealously watched the French become more powerful, for the French found the "gold" the Spanish had overlooked —they quickly realized the value of furs, America's greatest source of wealth during the next two hundred years. They traded cheap knives, whisky, blunderbuss guns, and beads to the Indians for the skins of beaver, marten, mink, and otter, and sent them back to France.

By 1680 there were eight hundred Frenchmen fur-trading out in the forests, following the rivers and Indian trails over the vast territory that is now Ohio, Wisconsin, Iowa, and Minnesota. In the later struggle for the fur trade the French had the advantage of easy travel, for they knew the best water routes and the ready-made Indian portage paths leading directly into the fur country. These portages were footpaths connecting rivers, over which canoes and baggage had to be carried by hand. One important route followed the upper St. Lawrence River inland and over the upper reaches of the Great Lakes. The two waterways were connected by a seven-mile portage path around Niagara Falls.

The famed French Jesuit missionaries, called by the Indians "Black Robes," followed the Indian trails into the wilderness, going by water wherever possible, as the Indians did, and using their portage paths. The first four Jesuits had come to Quebec in 1625, and after the troubles with England were over some seven years later, many more priests crossed the ocean to carry the Church's word into the new wilderness country. These missionaries, straining to cross the rough northern trails of the Iroquois, wearily called them "roads of iron."

Protestant missionaries, too, came over from Europe, exploring the Indian trails and learning the Indian ways. The Indians must have been bewildered by these invasions of their ancient trails. Archer Hulbert, in the book *Indian Thoroughfares,* tells of an old Seneca chief who stood, deep in the forest, looking in wonder at a white man, a Moravian missionary. "Whither is the paleface going?" he asked. "Why does the paleface travel such unknown roads? This is no road for white people and no white man has come this trail before."

But the white men would not be stopped. Gradually, from bits of information put together like a jigsaw puzzle, they began to form an idea of the geography of the continent, of where the rivers ran and where the mountains rose.

Meanwhile, little English and Dutch villages grew up along the Atlantic coastline—Jamestown, Williamsburg, Philadelphia, New York, Boston. In them lived people with a different idea, who came not to explore or convert or trade but to stay, building solid houses for their families and planting crops. Unlike the French and Spanish, who thought of the red men as subjects of their kings, the English treated them as independent peoples with whom they made treaties and from whom they bought land.

Because only dangerous Indian trails connected

the colonies by land, the villages were truly iso-
lated—they were closer to Europe than to each other.
Differences in local customs, clothes, and even in the
manner of speaking grew more pronounced each
year because of the wilderness barriers. Only those
who had urgent business in another colony, or poor
families seeking better homes dared to travel the
"blind" Indian paths. But as the colonies grew, some
means of communication became imperative. In
time rough country roads were made, usually out-
growths of old trails, and travel on wheels developed
slowly between villages.

Another kind of travel became important—travel
away from the villages. This movement was
prompted partly by economic reasons, and partly by
the restlessness of footloose people in a strange, unsettled country. There have always been, and always
will be, people who want to see what is over the next
hill or what is around the bend in the river; and lack
of roads cannot keep such wanderers from pushing
on. This restlessness, coupled with the fact that
coastal villages were becoming crowded as more and
more settlers arrived from Europe, urged many people away from their tight little colonies.

Before long, English, German, and Scotch-Irish
settlers were moving away over the Indian paths
into what they themselves called the "howling

wilderness." They built rude log houses and lived by hunting, fishing, and trading; their clothes were half-European, half-Indian with deerskin jackets, coonskin caps, and moccasins. They were the "Borderers," living on the very frontier of civilization. And these early pioneers were called borderers in their own time, never backwoodsmen, a name in more popular use today.

The borderers had rich furs to trade, and later on cattle and horses for sale. But they needed salt, iron, and household goods from the East, and because of this need and because there were no roads to the border, a new era in American history was begun. This was the era of the pack horse.

These sturdy animals had been bred by crossing the Indian pony, which the Spaniards had brought over, with the "brave fat horses" of the Pennsylvania Dutch country. Each year in the fall, border families pooled their furs and sent them by pack-horse caravan over the mountains for barter in the East. The caravans followed the Indian trails along the high mountain ridges. A master driver was chosen, with two or three young men to help him. The drivers carried their own food, usually boiled ham, bread, and cheese. Around the horses' necks were hung feed bags filled with the animals' food, part of which had to be cached along the trail for the return trip, since eighty-five pounds of alum salt for the borderers was loaded in each feed bag on the way back.

Along the trail the pack horses moved in single file, each tied to the pack-saddle of the animal in front, with the driver leading the first in line. At night the animals were hobbled and turned loose. They wore bells around their necks so they could be heard easily, and after dark these were "opened," as the pioneers used to say, meaning the daytime stuffing was taken out of them.

Increasing numbers of pack-horse caravans made their way over the mountains as the ranks of borderers grew. But the colonies were growing fast in the 1700's, and more efficient transport was needed. Farm products from the border had to be brought to market. More tools and food and clothing from the East had to be delivered in return to the borders; and moreover, there were businessmen in the East who wanted their share of trade with the "far Indians," trade in the rich furs that had been finding their way to Montreal and Quebec and then to France.

A better way of transport was needed, a way on wheels. And for anything on wheels, real roads to the West were needed. But always, in the history of travel and transportation, the vehicle has come first, and beaten out its own road. As early as 1725, years before the pack-horse caravans had reached their full importance, the vehicle that would replace them was having its small beginning.

This was the Conestoga wagon, built first for use on the rich farms in the Conestoga Valley of Pennsylvania. During the next 150 years this wagon, or adaptations of it, with its canvas-covered top, was to haul all of the freight and most of the people going westward over the mountains.

The wagons, rolling only through well-settled country, at first met the pack-horse trains where the roads ended. But as the wagons ventured farther each year, the roads they used became wider and, of course, longer. The old pack-horse paths became shorter and less-used, for the caravans were picking out new trails in the West.

Pack horses, carrying from 150 to 200 pounds at best, could not compare in convenience and economy with the one- or two-ton covered wagons. Their day would end, but not until there were enough roads for wagons to cover the same distance. Even by the time of the Revolutionary War there were frequently as many as five hundred pack horses in a single caravan heading west from Carlisle, Pennsylvania, a central point. Picking their way over Indian trails and buffalo traces, the pack-horse caravans were a vital part of American life for more than a hundred years.

3. ROLLING ROADS

Goin' down town,
Goin' down town,
Goin' down to Richmond town
To carry my 'bacco down.

Old Virginia slave song

Virginia was the first of the colonies to anticipate the need for good roads. As early as 1632, only twenty-five years after the founding of Jamestown, the Virginia House of Burgesses passed a law requiring every man in the colony to get out on the road and work a certain number of days each year, or pay someone else to do the work for him if he didn't want to cut down trees and uproot stumps himself. This early act set the pattern for road laws in the colonies.

But good roads were a long time coming in the South. They were scarcely needed at first, because of the rivers. The southern colonist, in looking for a place to settle, considered two things of equal importance: good soil and a deep river, just as a farmer today settles where there is good soil and a good road.

The early Virginia planters stayed close to the ocean, and for nearly a hundred years the Blue

Ridge Mountains remained a mystery to them. They heard tales of the mountains from occasional Indians, hunters, and traders, but few colonists had seen them. Yet, though they did not know it, the Appalachian ranges set not only the courses of the rivers, but also the future of the southern colonies. They rose as a great barrier cutting off the South from the profitable fur trade of the Mississippi Valley. They slowed down the development of manufacture as well as of roads, and it was partly because of this that the South became a region of plantations.

The first plantations were built on the banks of the wide rivers which are so close to the Atlantic Ocean that their waters rise and fall with the sea tides. Because of these tidal rivers—the Potomac, the Rappahannock, the York, and the James—that part of Virginia and Maryland, the earliest to be settled, became known as "Tidewater."

That large inland sea, the Chesapeake Bay, stretched eastward from Virginia almost into Pennsylvania, and southward to within a few miles of North Carolina. Farther south there were more rivers: the Elizabeth, the Cooper, the Savannah, and thousands of smaller tidal streams and bays. These were the "roads" of the planters, and they were traveled as country roads are today—to go visiting, or to church, or into town to shop, or to haul farm products. Ocean-going ships, most of them from England, sailed these rivers, bringing visitors and goods to the colonists and returning loaded with rice from Charleston, tobacco from Virginia and Maryland, and sons from all three to be educated in England. The plantations were equipped with their own wharves, so for almost a century no real ports were needed.

By 1729 more than three hundred tobacco ships were crossing the Atlantic Ocean, back and forth between England and the river plantations. Great round hogsheads of tobacco, weighing from eight hundred to a thousand pounds, would be rolled from the storage or packing place on the plantation into the hold of the ship bound for England. Usually this work was done by slaves, but in the days before many slaves had been brought to Virginia and Maryland, the ships' crews rolled the tobacco down to the wharves. It was backbreaking work, and many an English sailor cursed the day he ever saw Virginia.

As the population of the Tidewater grew, tobacco planters settled the peninsulas between the rivers. They had to get their tobacco to the wharves in some way, and wherever possible they used the old Indian trails, chopping down trees and clearing away underbrush to make way for the massive hogsheads. Where no suitable trail existed, new roads leading directly to the wharves were cut through the forests. These were called "rolling roads" because the tobacco hogsheads were rolled over them. Many roads in Virginia today follow a roundabout course, because they were once rolling roads winding along the easiest way, skirting rivers and circling hills.

Spring and fall of the year were "rolling" times. Often the slaves and the overseer from one plantation would join those from another along the roads. They slept in the woods at night, their clothes covered with red mud from the half-finished roads.

Later someone had the idea of strapping canoes together to float tobacco to the wharves, and this method was followed wherever water travel was possible. It was much easier than rolling, for as many as ten hogsheads of tobacco at a time could be transported in this way. The canoes, in turn, gave way to the bateau, a strange-looking river craft something like a canoe, raised at the bow and stern.

Meanwhile, the Piedmont country at the foot of the Virginia mountains had become well settled. This section was too far away from water to roll tobacco, and other crops were raised—crops that could not be rolled without great damage to them. New roads were made for wagons and the old rolling roads were cleared of stumps and straightened. The wagons at first forded the small streams; later they crossed on ferries, and finally rumbled over rude bridges.

Before wagons appeared, farmers adapted for

their use a vehicle hewn from forest timber. This was the large, topheavy cart with two high wooden wheels, pulled by oxen. These carts lumbered so slowly over the rough trails that sometimes, when the load was heavy, they did not seem to move at all. But they were useful, for only a precipice or a deep bog in the road could stop them. Although wagons soon replaced oxcarts for distance hauling, the carts were used for years on farms and plantations.

Once the roads were built, town merchants began using them. They pulled their wagons up to the country stores, and bartered with the storekeepers for corn, wheat, or flour, products which had been brought in by farmers who used them in trade instead of money. Some merchants sent their Negro drivers out with a six- or eight-mule team pulling the wagon. These skilled drivers seldom used reins; but they knew how to cry "Gee!" and "Haw!" to keep balky mules moving over the muddy, rough roads. Merchants who did not have their own wagons and drivers hired wagoners who charged for hauling by the bushel, and according to the distance and condition of the road.

On passable roads horses often sank into sticky mud up to their knees, and when the snow melted in the mountains and the spring rains came, the "back country" roads could not be traveled at all for several weeks. During these times, merchants at

Charleston in South Carolina, Frederick and Bladensburg in Maryland, Georgetown on the Potomac, and Winchester and Richmond in Virginia looked up at darkening skies and wondered if their wagons would come through. Even the sturdy oxcart sometimes got stuck. Many museums today have these old oxcarts on display, and the gouges on the solid wooden wheels are proof that the roads they traveled over were rough indeed.

4. THE BOSTON POST ROAD

Where is the postman, Nancy, with the New England mail?
How slow he was a-coming, along the Indian trail.
And some poor fellows never came in; in solitude they fell
Before the savage tomahawk, with none to tell the tale.

Old poem by John H. Yates

Since in New England, too, the first settlements were on rivers and bays, water travel was the easiest means of getting about. But there had to be some means of land travel, for the population was growing rapidly and moving farther back, away from the water. By 1641, twenty thousand people lived in New England, in clusters of separate little communities.

Indian trails were used more and more as the years passed. There is a splendid sound to the names of these ancient paths—the Iroquois Trail, leading along the Hudson and Niagara rivers; the Old Connecticut Path, to Boston and Albany; the Kittanning Path, leading out of Philadelphia and over the mountains; the Scioto-Monongahela Trail in Ohio; and the great western trail, the Cuyahoga-Muskinghum.

As early as 1633 sixty men, women, and children traveled along the Connecticut Path, in search of better homes in the Connecticut River Valley. Little by little old stumps, rocks, and fallen branches were cleared from the trails, and notches cut on trees to blaze the way. Most traveling was done on foot, for the few horses were usually needed to work the farms. In time, however, the colonists evolved a method by which a number of people could use one horse to travel over the Indian trails. This was called "riding and tying." One couple would ride a horse a certain distance, tie it to a tree, and then go on by foot. The people behind them would reach the horse, climb into the saddle, ride along the trail, pass their friends on foot, and then tie up the horse when their turn was over. By riding and tying everybody got a chance to rest from walking—including the horse.

Gradually, as a spider's web is spun, the paths spread through all New England. And slowly, year by year, they became wider. After more than a hundred years had passed, there were rough roads for carts and wagons.

The government tried to help. In 1639 the Massachusetts General Court passed a law providing for a road to be built between Plymouth and Boston. This small stretch of road became a part of one of the most famous early highways in America, the Boston Post Road, which connected Boston and New York.

It is now a part of the famous Route 1, which follows the Atlantic coastline from Maine to Florida.

Along the 250 miles of the Boston Post Road sped America's first regular post riders, or mail carriers. The first post rider galloped out of New York with the northbound mail January 22, 1673, on a mission from the Governor of New York to create good-will and understanding between the two settlements. Speeding along the Boston Post Road when it was only a horse trail, this first mailman in America took three weeks to get to Boston from New York. The postal service was discontinued for a few years because of disputes with the Dutch over New York, and war with the Indians in New England. By 1685 mail service over the Boston Post Road was renewed, and the horseback deliveries continued without interruption until the Revolutionary War.

Summer's heat, dust, and mud, and winter's snow, sleet, rain, and bitter cold were the least of the difficulties faced by those first hard-riding mailmen, alone on the forest paths. Galloping a horse on so rough a trail might mean injury or death to animal or rider at any misstep, and there was always the possibility of attack by Indians, for the unsettled wilderness lay close to the doors of towns in those days. Many a rider ended his journey dead by the side of the road, his mail blown about by the winds.

Within a few years the post riders were on a

twice-a-week schedule, one saddling up and starting out from Boston on the same day that another set out from New York. Galloping toward each other along the old Boston Post Road, they met at a tavern about halfway, probably near Saybrook, Connecticut. Here the New Yorker handed the Boston rider the two saddlebags of mail for New England, and the Bostonian gave him the New York mail. A meal, a brief rest, a hearty wish for good luck, and each started off for home.

Slowly the mail service reached out. By 1717 post riders made regular trips between Boston and Williamsburg, the early capital of Virginia. Mail was delivered once a month in summer and once every two months in winter. In less than a hundred years after the first post rider galloped off from New York with the New England mail, letters could be sent from Boston as far south as Charleston, South Carolina. In the spring of 1763 Benjamin Franklin, the colonial postmaster, made an inspection of the posts in his charge, riding over the rough roads in a one-horse chaise, or "shay." His daughter accompanied him, traveling most of the way on horseback. One year later Franklin started day-and-night mail service over the Boston Post Road—he used to boast that he could send a letter from Philadelphia to Boston and get a reply in three weeks! A fast-growing country needed fast mails.

In the early eighteenth century, wagons began to appear along the Boston Post Road hauling freight from city to city, but many more years passed before any public passenger service was established between Boston and New York. The first stagecoach service was begun in 1772, but it didn't last long; coach travel from Boston stopped when the Revolutionary War broke out.

The most traveled roads of the time were those connecting the largest towns, Boston, New York, Philadelphia, and Baltimore. There were no good roads at all, as we think of them today. In wet weather they were rivers of mud; in dry weather their whole lengths were clouded with dust. Busy with planting and harvesting in spring, summer, and fall, the colonists usually did their traveling in the winter, when they could go by horse-drawn sleigh over snow-covered roads. And all travel was slow; George Washington, rushing from Philadelphia to Boston to take command of the Continental Army in 1775, was twelve days on the road!

At the time of the Revolution the only settled area in America was a strip of land along the coast and in the Shenandoah Valley, extending west no more than 150 miles. (Many people had already moved beyond the Alleghenies, but these were the borderers relying on pack horses for trade with the settled communities.) The main roads connecting towns ran in a north-and-south direction. People who traveled any long distance usually made their way on foot or horseback at an average speed of four miles an hour. A traveler could buy a horse along the way, ride to the next town, sell the horse there, and buy another to continue his journey. However, very few people traveled at all, and many never ventured more than twenty miles away from home.

For years after the Revolution, stagecoach travel over the Boston Post Road was slight. During Washington's first term as President twelve horses and two stages handled all the stagecoach traffic—both passenger and freight—over the Boston Post Road. The early public coaches, bumping along behind the horses, had no springs at all, and only hard wooden seats for passengers. Later the body of the coach was hung on leather straps, which made travel slightly more comfortable. The vehicles were called "stage-coaches" because the journey was made in stages, from place to place, where the tired horses were changed for fresh ones.

It took a courageous person to travel by stage-coach then, and many men drew up their wills before starting on such a journey. There was the danger of overturned coaches and upset ferries, and long waits while coach and horses were pulled out of the mud. Passengers, shaken miserably like pills in a tight box, were hot and choked with dust in summer, and freezing cold in winter. They found little time for rest in the taverns, for they were routed out of their beds at two or three o'clock in the morning, rain or shine. Eighteen dangerous, uncomfortable hours were spent on each lap of the journey; it took six days to reach New York from Boston.

A new nation was rising, and it needed fine roads and better vehicles to connect its towns. And, even without real roads, people were beginning to move westward. Some families rode over the old military road cut from an Indian trail by British General Braddock during the war against the French. This rugged wilderness road ran, when completed, 110 miles from Cumberland, Maryland, to Pittsburgh, Pennsylvania. Rude trails converged at the two outpost towns. At the Ohio River, the pioneers built rafts and floated downstream, seeking new homes not too close to Indians. Pennsylvanians journeyed deeper into the interior, piling their household goods and tools on flatboats, and slowly poling them along the Susquehanna River. Others, by wagon and pack-train, drove through the Mohawk Valley to make new homes in the unsettled regions of upper New York.

More roads, roads going west, were needed for all the people who wanted to push farther on into wilderness country.

5. THE WILDERNESS ROAD

In a few years more, those of us who are alive will move off to Kaintuck or the Mississippi, where corn can be had for six pence a bushel and pork for a penny a pound. I do not wonder at the rage for emigration. What do the bulk of the people get here that they cannot have there for one-fifth the labor in the western country.

John Randolph (1813)

In between Indian-held lands in long stretches of the southern forests and the vast territory along the Ohio River was "no man's land," called by the Iroquois Ken-ta-kee, "among the meadows." It was a beautiful country where thousands of buffalo, deer, and other game roamed. But there were rivals for this rich land, and so many battles had been fought for it, so many Indians had died trying to gain it, that it had another name: "The dark and bloody ground."

This was Kentucky. No roads led into it—there was only a mountain slash called Cumberland Gap, and through it ran the Warrior's Path, vanishing into the wilderness. Few white hunters and traders had ventured in, and of those who did many never saw a white man's face again. In New England, coaches were rolling along the post roads, and Conestoga wagons were rumbling their way over the mountains in Pennsylvania; but little was known of the wilderness country that is now Kentucky.

In 1769, with two companions, Daniel Boone left his frontier home in western North Carolina and traveled into Kentucky. A trader had told him of the wonderful game there, and of the rich soil. He and his companions were captured by the Shawnees, but escaped; the Indians later recaptured one of his friends and killed him, and the other returned to civilization with his hard-won furs and other bounty. But Boone stayed on alone in Kentucky for two years, exploring, living by his rifle, hunting and being hunted. He knew the country then as well as the Indians had ever known it, and he wanted to bring his family and make his home in this land of rich earth and roaming game.

For two more years Boone worked to gather colonists for his promised land. Finally the party was ready: forty men, women, and children, driving before them grunting swine and herds of cattle into the wilderness over the Warrior's Path. At Cumberland Gap Boone sent his seventeen-year-old son James with a small group to bring up a family waiting to join the settlers. Indians attacked the little group, killing all but two of them. The settlers turned back, guessing rightly that an Indian war was beginning. Daniel Boone's dream would have to wait.

Meanwhile, the Transylvania Company had been formed. Its aim was to develop Kentucky—twenty million acres of it. The Cherokees owned the land, since the Iroquois had given up their claim under the Treaty of Fort Stanwix in 1768, and the company wanted Daniel Boone to buy the land from them and open up a road into the wilderness for settlers. It was the Company's plan then to sell parcels of the land to the settlers.

With ten wagons loaded with red shirts, old muskets, mirrors, and trinkets—ten thousand pounds of goods in all—Daniel Boone bought the rights of the Cherokees to Kentucky for the Transylvania Company. Twelve thousand Cherokee warriors, their squaws and papooses, and twelve painted chiefs attended the pow-wow. Feasting, speech-making, and arguing finally ended, and Kentucky passed into the white man's hands. It was then that one of the chiefs turned to Boone and said: "Brother, it is good land we have sold you but you will find it hard to hold."

The Indian chief was right. It was hard land to hold, and it was hard land to get into, for first a road had to be hacked through the wilderness. This, too, was Daniel Boone's job.

In the spring of 1775, with thirty men or so, carrying rifles to shoot game and axes to chop trees and underbrush, Daniel Boone set out to open a way into the new land for the settlers who would follow. From Watauga, the site of the pow-wow, the road led straight to the Cumberland Gap, where Kentucky, Tennessee, and Virginia come together. From the Gap they followed the Warrior's Path for fifty miles northward, clearing underbrush, cutting down trees, blazing the way for others to come. Leaving the Warrior's Path, they veered to the west and followed a buffalo trace from Hazel Patch. The road was pushed on to the Rockcastle River.

The forest growth became more and more difficult for the road builders after leaving the buffalo trace. For twenty miles they cut their way through dead brush and then through thick cane and weed in what is now Madison County, Kentucky. Finally they pushed through the canebrake and saw the beautiful plains of the country, Daniel Boone's promised land. A member of the party, Felix Walker, spoke of it as "a new sky and a strange earth."

When they were within fifteen miles of the site that had been chosen for the settlement, Indians attacked. They tore into the sleeping camp, shooting from the woods, swinging tomahawks. The road builders grabbed their rifles and rushed into the dark forest to fight from cover. Captain William Twitty, shot through both knees, could not move. His bulldog leaped at the Indian attacking his master and knocked him down. Another red man rushed in and killed the dog, then both Indians vanished. Both Twitty and his Negro slave died in the attack, two men were badly wounded, and all were terrified. They wanted to turn back, and would have but for Daniel Boone, who would not give up.

After the Wilderness Road was cut through the forest Boonesborough was built, and pioneer settlers used the road to enter Kentucky. Two of them, Boone's wife Rebecca and daughter Jemima, were the first white women in Kentucky. In the years that followed the war a constant stream of pioneers traveled over the Wilderness Road into Kentucky, driving their tired cattle before them, urging along the pack horses which carried their household goods.

The Wilderness Road was perhaps the most desperately gained and hard-fought-for road in the history of our country—and one of the most important. Only fifteen years after its completion there were seventy thousand people in Kentucky! By 1800 more than 220,000 people lived in the land that so recently had been a wilderness.

Daniel Boone, hunter, woodsman, Indian-fighter, had made the settlement of the new land possible; but he didn't like so many people around him. "Old woman," he said to his wife, "we must move. They are crowding us." And so, in 1798, the Boones left for Spanish lands in Missouri.

NEW FRONTIERS

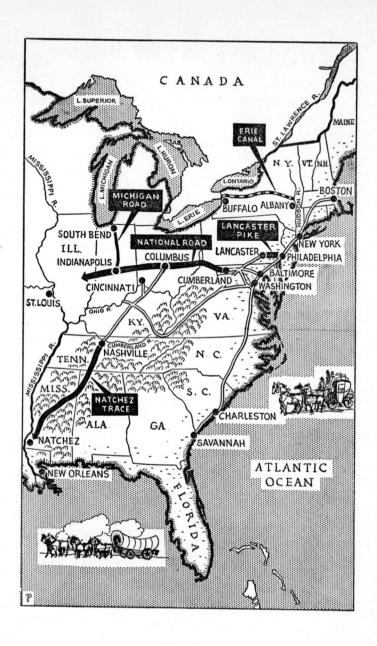

6. THE LANCASTER PIKE

Many a fleet of them,
In one long, upward winding row.
It ever was a noble sight
As from the distant mountain height
Or quiet valley far below,
Their snow-white covers looked like sail.

Old poem by David Eby

Business in the new country, the United States, was humming as the 1700's drew to a close. Heavily laden sailing packets made their way up and down the coast between New England and the South, and along the coast by land Conestoga wagons hauled their freight over the rutted, muddy roads.

Covered wagons, in general use since 1750, had by this time been built to suit the needs of overland hauling, and were called freighters. A team of six horses pulled them, and these, with the length of wagon, spread out to sixty feet. The white canvas cover alone was twenty-four feet long. The Conestogas, carrying loads of from two to four tons, were the backbone of trade.

But the flow of goods was beginning to take another direction—into the East from the growing western settlements. New York and Philadelphia were eager for the goods from the rich frontier, and while it was fairly easy for wagons to get in and out of New York, the Appalachian Mountains lay between Philadelphia and the frontier. They formed a three-thousand-foot-high barrier cutting off Pennsylvania businessmen from the farmers of the western country. When New York began to get most of the trade, there was only one answer for Pennsylvania—to build a road to the West.

In the spring of 1792 the state of Pennsylvania gave permission to the Philadelphia and Lancaster Turnpike Road Company to build a road, a *good* road, connecting Philadelphia and Lancaster, sixty-two miles away. With its fine wheat farms, fat cattle, and sleek horses, Lancaster was the breadbasket of the coastal regions. It was also the largest town in the United States not situated on water, a meeting place for roads from the South and West, and the end of the journey for pack-horse caravans making their way over the mountains. From this center the traffic of several trade routes could pour into Philadelphia.

The Lancaster Turnpike road was the first extensive, planned road in the United States, and it was the first good road of any importance. Constructed of broken limestone and gravel, it lay twenty-four feet wide, with a long grassy slope bordering each side. The passing traffic would not make ruts in it, but would instead pack it down more firmly.

Two years of hard work and 465,000 dollars went into the building of the turnpike. One fine three-arch bridge across Brandywine Creek alone cost twelve thousand dollars. It was not a free road, for it had not been built by the government. Private citizens put money into the turnpike company to finance the road, and they expected to make money out of it. This they did, for soon after its opening in 1794 the Lancaster-Philadelphia Turnpike was doing a booming business. It was so much more satisfactory than the old hit-or-miss dirt roads, people didn't mind paying the toll.

The road was operated on a pay-as-you-go system. A gate, in the form of a long pole studded with pikes, blocked the entrance to the highway until the traveler had paid the first of the toll charges, when it was swung out of the way. Because of this type of gate pay-roads became known as "turnpikes." There were nine toll gates in all, spaced about seven miles apart, and at each of these a toll was charged. The rate varied from one cent to thirteen and one-half cents per mile, depending on the width of the wheels and the number of horses used.

The well-to-do traveler journeyed by stagecoach, which sped along behind six spanking horses. Inside the coach passengers sat comfortably on cushioned seats, peering from behind the silken draperies at the windows. Special taverns along the Pike catered to stagecoach travelers, providing the best of food and comfortable beds. The taverns became the meeting-places of people living nearby, places where the latest news from the cities came first-hand to country-dwelling Pennsylvanians. It was a coach which carried the announcement along the Lancaster Pike that the second war with England, the War of 1812, was finally over. The news was written in large letters on a white muslin band wrapped around the top of the coach.

Conestoga wagons glittered in the sunlight along the Lancaster Pike. They were all painted alike, the enormous underbody of the wagon blue, the upper body red, the curving canvas top a gleaming white. These patriotic colors were appropriate, for in their day Conestoga wagons hauled the entire freight of the young country's growing commerce.

At regular points along the Pike freight packing-houses were situated, and here the big wagons were loaded and packed with great care. The curve of the top of the wagon, front and back, prevented the tons of freight from sliding out when going up or down hill. The drivers of the Conestogas were strong men—they had to be strong to hold six horses in rein, and guide a wagon weighing tons. They were a clannish, tight-knit group, bound together by their common disdain for the handsomely dressed stage-coach drivers and the landlords whose fine taverns were not for them. They had their own taverns, called "wagonhouses."

Day after day they guided their red, white, and blue wagons into the West, rolling down the Lancaster Pike with their cargos of nails, farm tools, household goods, clothing, sugar, and other eastern supplies needed by the faraway settlers and the even more remote borderers. At the end of the Pike the goods were unloaded and packed on small wagons, carts, and pack horses to be driven over the mountains and down to the valley of the Ohio River. From the settlers the Conestogas brought back flour, grain, salt, pork, bacon, and farm produce for eastern markets.

The expression "I'll be there with bells on" probably originated in the days of the Conestoga wagons. From an iron ring attached to the collar of one of the horses were hung a half-dozen or more bells, clanging symbols of self-reliance, for it was the custom that the bells be surrendered to anyone who supplied help when the wagon broke down.

Besides the coaches and the Conestoga wagons, there was another kind of traffic on the Lancaster Pike: the movement of people which would one day push the last frontier to the Pacific Ocean. Along the road streamed families seeking new homes in the western settlements, their wagons piled high with furniture and the tools to build homes and start farms, with often a sad-eyed family cow bringing up the rear.

Such was the Lancaster Pike, the first hard-surfaced road in the United States. It served the very beginning of heavy cross-country commerce in America. The United States capitol was then rising on a hill in Washington, and the young nation was feeling its first real growth; it needed many more roads like the Lancaster Pike. To be sure, the Pike did not go very far westward as we think of miles today, but it was a good start, the first link in the chain of good roads to come.

7. THE NATCHEZ TRACE

And if a daring foe annoys
  No matter what his force is,
We'll show him that Kentucky boys
  Are Alligator-Horses.
        Song of Mississippi boatmen

The lower Mississippi Valley, called "the Spanish fringe," was under the rule of Spain in the late 1700's. The people were French, English, and Spanish, or half-and-half, or a mixture of all three.

Although so different in culture and life, the American and Spanish frontiers were friendly, trading with each other by way of the great Mississippi River. Natchez, Mississippi, with a few hundred people, was the northernmost settlement on Spanish land; Nashville, Tennessee, somewhat larger, was the nearest American village. Between these two frontier towns stretched five hundred miles of wilderness. It was Indian country. The only means of travel between the towns was over an ancient path, which in its time served as one of the most important factors in the development of the United States. This trail, called the "Natchez

Trace," was for many years the only land route to the new southwest; but even during the period of its greatest use, it remained a wilderness path.

Thousands of buffalo first beat out this trace between the swamplands of the Mississippi River and the salt licks in Tennessee where Nashville now stands. Then the Choctaw Indians, the sun-worshipping Natchez, and the war-making Chickasaws used the trail, extending it over highlands and between watersheds. For many years it was known as the "Chickasaw Path." De Soto, in his search for gold, followed this path through the wilderness. When Americans began to use it, they called it the "Natchez Trace."

In 1796 the first post rider on the Trace carried his mail south from Nashville, urging his horse through swamps and tangled forest. A few years later, when the United States bought the Louisiana Territory from France, President Jefferson ordered his Secretary of War to make a treaty with the Indians for the improvement of their ancient path. Perhaps Jefferson wanted only to smooth the way for the benefit of commercial travelers; perhaps he anticipated the inevitable expansion and wanted the Natchez Trace ready for the thousands of pioneers who would follow it to the new Southwest Territory, and on to Texas.

The Natchez Trace became important because of one simple fact: it's easy to float down a long, powerful river, but hard and slow work to row or pole a boat upstream against the current; in the days before steam power, a boatman could make better time walking home. The return path of the Mississippi River boatmen was the Natchez Trace.

Actually, the story of this southern road begins far to the north. West of the Allegheny mountains, frontier towns were humming. Millers, weavers, printers, ropemakers, brickmakers, and other skilled workmen were manufacturing goods in these towns. Farmers brought in from their barnyards and fields fat cattle and pigs and large crops for sale. The towns in the river valleys became important trading centers, especially Louisville, Cincinnati, and Pittsburgh—but the really big markets were in the East. How could the slow, clumsy pack-horse caravans carry to the eastern states all the goods from this vast region? Even after Conestoga wagons pushed over the mountains, travel was slow and freight rates high. Farmers tried driving their cattle over the mountains to Philadelphia, but the trip took months and the animals arrived thin and half-starved.

Another way had to be found—and the townsmen discovered they could float goods down the Ohio and Mississippi rivers to New Orleans, and thence by sea to the coastal cities. They used anything that would stay afloat—keelboats, barges, rafts, and finally "flatboats."

The flatboats that floated down the Mississippi River to New Orleans were really large rafts, guided fore and aft by boatmen using long-handled rudders to steer by. Perched in the center was a small cabin for the crew. The deck in front and behind the cabin was piled high with cargo bound for a southern port that might be more than a thousand miles away—cotton, sugar, flour, bacon, salt pork, lard, dried fruits, cider, salt, iron.

The trip was slow, of course, but not so costly as the mountain route, even though there was no return for the flatboats. At New Orleans the rivermen sold not only their goods, but also their flatboats, broken up for lumber. A few adventurers shipped on sailing boats for foreign ports, but most of the flatboat-men were farmers bringing their produce to market; they had to make their own way home afoot. Others were rivermen who returned to home base to pick up another downstream load.

The professional rivermen who steered clumsy flatboats over the treacherous Mississippi were wild, rough, strong men. Half-rivermen, half-landsmen, they called themselves "alligator-horses." Alexander Wilson, the famous ornithologist, who saw a group of

them start off from Natchez in 1810, described them
in this manner:

> As dirty as Hottentots; their dress a shirt and
> trowsers of canvass, black, greasy, and sometimes
> in tatters; the skin burnt wherever exposed to the
> sun; each with a budget, wrapt up in an old blan-
> ket; their beards, eighteen days old added to the
> singularity of their appearance which was alto-
> gether savage.

The men who were "half a horse and half an alligator" did indeed have a savage look about them;
but they had a quietness, too—the relaxed alertness
of men who must always be ready for danger.

The rivermen and farmers usually banded together in groups of fifteen or twenty for the return
trip, for it was dangerous to travel the Natchez Trace
alone. Not from the Indians themselves—treaties had
been made with them—but from outlaws, both
white and Indian, hiding in the canebrake, there
was the risk of robbery and even death. The most
hated and feared brigand was Samuel Mason, who
with his two sons and seven or eight other men
formed a terrifying band. Sometimes they preyed
on river craft, but not often—Mason was said to brag
as he watched the flatboats drifting down the river,

"They are taking produce to the market for me."

In the early years no taverns offered food and shelter on the Natchez Trace. The rivermen and farmer-traders carried their own food: rice, dried beef, bacon, flour, coffee, and a kind of biscuit made by a Spanish baker in the fort of Natchez, which was something like hardtack and which they called "travelers' bread." Good shots could bring down turkey or bag deer, and some knew how to find sweet wild honey; but toward the end of the long stretch many travelers kept alive each day on small portions of pulverized Indian corn.

Hurricanes and snowstorms sometimes swept over the Natchez Trace. In wet weather, swamps and creeks overflowed, and horses sank in the water up to their saddlebags; some of them sank so deep they couldn't be pulled out of the stiff clay bottoms and were left to die. The men built campfires at night to keep away bears and wolves which prowled the wild country.

In hot weather the travelers rose with the sun, packed their horses, and continued until eleven o'clock, or until they found water. Then they rested for a few hours before pushing on until sundown. The only break in the long journey was at the Chickasaw villages where the friendly Indians occasionally offered tired rivermen corn and fresh milk. Beyond the villages there was only wilderness

The Spanish, who came to America early in the sixteenth century, were the first white men to dare the new wilderness. They named their network of trails *Los Caminos Reales*—The Royal Highways.

Indian portage paths provided ready-made transportation for French explorers, fur trappers, and missionaries. The black-robed Jesuits, trudging wearily over the rough paths, called them "roads of iron."

In 1633 sixty men, women, and children traveled the Connecticut Path in search of new homesteads. By "riding and tying" they devised an ingenious way of alternating horse- and foot-travel.

Great round hogsheads of tobacco, some of them weighing a thousand pounds, were rolled by slaves from storage houses into the holds of ships bound for England. The roads they used were called "rolling roads."

One of the most famous early highways in history, the Boston Post Road, connected New York and Boston. It is now a part of Route 1, the great artery which follows the Atlantic coastline from Maine to Florida.

Forerunner of today's streamliner was "The Flying Machine," in truth only a springless (and most uncomfortable) wagon, but which boasted a run of a day and a half between New York and Philadelphia.

Through cane and brush and Indian attacks Daniel Boone and his men blazed Kentucky's Wilderness Road—perhaps the most desperately gained roadway in America, and certainly one of the most important.

The Lancaster Turnpike was operated on a pay-as-you-go system. A long pole studded with pikes blocked the highway until the traveler paid his toll—thus the name "turnpike" for pay roads.

Until the coming of steamboats, the Natchez Trace served as the up-river route of the rivermen, or "alligator horses." It was a desolate, dangerous path of swamp and forest and highwaymen.

By 1802 stagecoaches were making regularly scheduled runs, connecting with each other at taverns all along the coast from Boston to Savannah. At breakneck speed, such a trip required more than three weeks.

From about 1788 until some time after steamboats traveled the interior rivers, an estimated million pioneers floated and poled their way to the growing cities of the new western country.

The Erie Canal, built at a cost of seven million dollars, provided a new gateway to the rich lands of the Middle West and started an era of feverish canal-building activity throughout the country.

In 1826 Indiana built a road for the thousands of settlers moving north-ward through the state. Called the Michigan Road, it was for many years the chief route between the Ohio River Valley and Lake Michigan.

Many early roads were privately financed, for the states could not afford to keep up with the demand; by charging tolls for the use of these roads, the investor quickly regained his interest in the venture.

For three years after the advent of railroads, competition ran high between steam- and horse-drawn cars. After various mishaps—including exploding engines—the "iron horse" eventually won out.

The National Road, built over the route of early pioneers, was America's first super-highway. Starting at Cumberland, Maryland, it led through Pennsylvania, Virginia, Ohio, Indiana, Illinois.

again for two hundred miles—in fact, until almost within sight of Nashville. The terrible journey took on an average three weeks.

Despite the dangers of the Natchez Trace, many of the alligator-horses chose to walk rather than spend fifty silver dollars for an Indian pony. Some of these became well known on the Natchez Trace as indomitable hikers; one man, nicknamed "Walking Johnson," boasted that he beat the post rider to Nashville three times!

At Nashville the boatmen usually broke up the party and went their separate ways, some traveling eastward over the Knoxville Trail, some northward through the Ohio country by Zane's Trace, others over Daniel Boone's Wilderness Road through Cumberland Gap.

Rude taverns, called "stands," began in time to appear on the Natchez Trace. They advertised that always on hand were "bacon, biscuit, etc., for the convenience of those going into the wilderness." John McCollum put up a sign between two china trees facing his stable: "Entertainment for man and baste."

The alligator-horses, farmers, and brave post riders were not the only travelers on the Trace. In 1809 Meriwether Lewis (of the Lewis and Clark exploring team) was mysteriously murdered at one of the taverns on the Natchez Trace. Lewis had been exploring the new territory for Thomas Jefferson, and was on his way to Washington to give his report to the President. Who murdered him—and why—is an unsolved mystery.

Four years after Lewis' death, soldiers dressed in homespun and buckskin hunting shirts were tramping northward over parts of the trail. These were Andrew Jackson's long-striding men. They were proud of their commander, pushing through the wilderness in his muddy boots, enduring all the hardships of the winter's march through the terrible country, watching unceasingly over his tired soldiers. He is supposed to have earned his nickname there when one of his soldiers remarked that he was "as tough as hickory."

Other people came: missionaries going into the new Southwest to bring their camp meetings and religion to settlers and Indians along the Mississippi River; men who had business in New Orleans, and those who journeyed for adventure. Even a few curious Europeans now and then traveled this wilderness path, and saw the growths of gray Spanish moss clinging to ancient oaks, the centuries-old Tulip trees, fragile dogwood, and the pink Judas tree.

Among the most important travelers over the Natchez Trace were hundreds of settlers from Kentucky, Tennessee, Virginia, and southern Ohio, making their way southward to the Mississippi River, and from there going on to Spanish lands farther west. Many of these men settled in Texas, and helped win that state from Mexico for the Union.

But after a time the ancient pathway was no longer needed. Steamboats began moving up the Mississippi River, so that flatboat-men could ride upstream in comfort, as did Abraham Lincoln when he and a friend took a flatboat loaded with produce down the Mississippi to New Orleans in 1828. They traveled a thousand miles and were away from home three months.

When the Trace was no longer a "through-route" between Natchez and Nashville, parts of it were improved for local use, and other long stretches abandoned to the creeping forests. Only once again in the nineteenth century was there any large movement on the Trace: years later both Union and Confederate soldiers tramped over the abandoned pathway during the Civil War.

Most American roads began as trails, were widened into wagon roads, and eventually became hard-surfaced highways. The Natchez Trace was an exception. Beginning as a trail perhaps a thousand or more years ago, it was used by white men for only a brief time; and during the period of its greatest importance it never became even a wagon road. Perhaps that is why, as the years passed, the abandoned trail became almost a legend, for all its history was of the past—a past of vanished buffalo, of Chickasaw, Natchez, and Choctaw Indians, of wild rivermen with their rawhide money bags, of outlaws, marching soldiers, and pioneers.

8. LONG ROADS NEAR
THE OCEAN

. . . the same bad roads and difficult rivers, connecting the same small towns, stretched into the same forests in 1800 as when the armies of Braddock and Amherst pierced the western and northern wilderness, except that these roads extended a few miles farther from the seacoast. Nature was rather man's master than his servant, and the five million Americans struggling with the untamed continent seemed hardly more competent to their task than the beavers and buffalo which had for countless generations made bridges and roads of their own.

Henry Adams

Travel today is a quite different matter from what it was to the Americans who lived 150 years ago, when the United States was young. The wretched condition of America's roads discouraged any but the most necessary journey, and except for adventurers and visiting Europeans, there was little if any travel for sightseeing; no sight would have been worth the pain.

Roads, which we take for granted today as we do the morning newspaper, were then of vital importance to the traveler. Strangers' greetings to each other were: "Good day, sir, and how is the road ahead?" and "Friend, how is it in your part of the country?" These were not merely polite questions. The traveler needed the answers. And the reply came with an equal courtesy and interest because the questioner had touched on a common need.

It was much as people have acted in any age when facing a common distress. Something stands, affecting them all; so they warm up and talk to any and all who mention it. The roads, thus, placed an imprint on the American character which persists to this day. The traveler who sticks his head from a car window and stopping someone on road or street inquires of his way ahead receives in overwhelming instance sympathetic treatment. Something else happened too: in the course of the talk of roads between the man from New England and the man from Virginia and Georgia other topics came up and thus the news of the day was spread and, more important, a kindredship of the American people.

Virginia had the first toll road in the United States—the Little River Turnpike—built in 1786 from the thriving port of Alexandria on the Potomac to Snigger's Gap across the mountains east of Winchester. Connecticut, Maryland, Pennsylvania, and Tennessee followed the road-building example, and in 1804 North Carolina cut a road through Cherokee Indian lands. So, although there were few planned highways in the early 1800's, long stretches of roads at least joined one another, and travel was possible all along the Atlantic Coast. However, the person who traveled for any distance reached his destination bone-weary, for only in short stretches were the roads in tolerably good condition.

All bridges were made of wood in the early days, and in 1800 the addition of trusses made higher and longer bridges possible. Frequently bridges were covered entirely, to protect the trusses and to keep horses from being frightened when high above a river or stream. Farther inland small stone piers bridged an occasional stream, and by the turn of the century a stone arched bridge began to appear. There were also floating bridges, made simply of heavy, thick planks held together by wooden stringers; these always sank a little under the weight of horses and coaches.

Almost all eastern travel overland was done in stagecoaches, offering the latest in "speed and luxury" to the public. Some roads were stone-surfaced like the Lancaster Pike, or "macadamized" after the manner of the Scotch road designer, McAdam; stage horses could go over these at a fast trot. Others —for hundreds of miles—were miserable dirt or "corduroy." The latter, made by placing tree trunks across the roadbed, had one advantage: they offered a surface firm enough to keep the coach or wagon from sinking in the mud. But the surface was so very uneven that after a time, from constant shaking, the wagon coach would fall apart! Sometimes, too, green boughs still attached to the tree-trunks tangled with the wagon wheels. The coaches would overturn, tumbling passengers in sprawling heaps and scattering and breaking the baggage tied to the top. The travelers were expected to be obliging and (provided they hadn't been hurt) to help the driver quiet the horses and get the coach back on its wheels. When the driver yelled back, "Gentlemen, to the right!" the gentlemen, and the ladies also, leaned in that direction to balance the tilting coach. Passengers on post lines knew very well that if the coach appeared hopelessly stuck, their driver might desert them, pick up the mail pouch, and carry it ahead on foot or by hitching a ride with a passing oxcart.

By 1802 stagecoaches were making regularly scheduled runs, connecting with each other at taverns all the way from Boston to Savannah, Georgia, twelve hundred miles away by stage route. A coastwise traveler went from Boston to New York in four days, and from there to Philadelphia in another day and a half, at a cost of fifteen dollars. He was on the road from Philadelphia to Charleston for fifteen long days, and paid fifty dollars for the experience. Another two days and five dollars more landed him in Savannah. Altogether, he spent nearly a hundred dollars, counting the cost for meals and lodging in taverns. With an average speed of fifty-three miles a day, the trip required more than three weeks. This was considered breakneck speed, however, and most people stopped over for a rest here and there at pleasant taverns.

In Louisiana, Mississippi, Alabama, and Georgia the roads were even worse than those of the middle Atlantic seaboard, and travel in the deep South remained hazardous until the coming of the railroads. Carl Arfwedson, a Swedish visitor to this country in the 1830's, morosely estimated in his book the chances of survival on a journey from Augusta, South Carolina, to New Orleans:

A traveller intending to proceed hence by land to New Orleans is earnestly recommended to bid adieu to all comforts on leaving Augusta, and make the necessary preparations for a hard and rough campaign. If he has a wife and children unprovided for, and to whom he has not the means of leaving a suitable legacy, let him by all means be careful to insure his life to the highest amount the offices will take; for the chances of perishing on the road are at the rate of ten to one, calculated according to the following table of casualties:

1 By horses running away.
2 By drowning.
3 By murder.
4 By explosion.

Arfwedson took his chance and arrived in the deep South safely, but had a bad experience on the journey, "hazarding his person in the woods of Georgia and Alabama":

It was towards dusk that I took my place in a narrow, old-fashioned stage, in company with eight passengers, who were proceeding to Macon, a distance of about one hundred and twenty-five miles. Scarcely had we lost sight of Augusta, when a dark, heavy cloud, greeted us with a drenching shower. All the luggage had, in consequence of the great quantity of mail-bags, been thrown carelessly on the top of the stage: let the reader judge of its condition at sunrise on the following morning, when our coach fairly stuck fast in a mud-hole, out of which the soaking wet and mud-covered passengers vainly endeavoured for several successive hours to extricate it. One of them, a foolish landlord, contributed materially to its extrication, and to keep up the spirits of his unfortunate travelling companions, by singing Irish melodies: but, desirous of accompanying his songs by an exhibition on the light fantastic toe, he suddenly slipped, and disappeared in the deep puddle, splashing the bystanders all over with dirty water. Owing to the coolness of the driver, he, however, escaped a watery grave; but, wet as he was, he resumed his seat inside the coach. Having at length obtained assistance from some waggoners, who with difficulty contrived to lift the stage out of the hole, we continued our journey . . . The road, entirely of clay, sadly cut up by the continual transport of cotton, and full of deep holes and furrows, had, besides, numberless roots, stumps, and trunks of trees, left absolutely untouched by the makers of this highway.

Along about midnight the coach wheels and pole were "shivered to pieces," and the party of eight, abandoning both coach and driver, struck out on foot through the "wild forest," arriving in Macon at daylight.

By 1812 there were 4,500 miles of roads in the eastern states, chartered and in operation, capitalized at 7,500,000 dollars. That year marked the beginning of the second war with England and roads to the South were used more than ever: with the fast sailing packets confined to harbor, all freight movement and travel had to be by land. During this time ten or twenty Conestoga wagons rumbled into

Charleston, South Carolina, daily, bringing goods from Richmond, Baltimore, Philadelphia, New York, and Boston.

But people wanted more roads. New industries were booming, interstate trade was growing, and the population was increasing rapidly. Why were good roads so slow in coming? Everybody knew better roads could be built—look at the Lancaster Pike. Look at the road the bankers of Baltimore had financed to Frederick. Look at the splendid New York–Philadelphia highway, and the road from Philadelphia to Pittsburgh! State lawmaking bodies were swamped with proposals for roads, roads, and more roads; Kentucky, nearly a hundred years ahead of most states, in 1821 established a State Highway Department. But the states were poor; and the federal government was so young and inexperienced, there was no real thought given to the idea that this country's roads should be under any kind of national control.

Some states found the answer in lotteries. Then, all over the country, private companies began building turnpikes. At first these companies got back their money—and more—by charging the public for the use of the roads. Every four or five miles along a privately owned turnpike a gatekeeper stopped the big Conestogas, the stagecoaches, and the small wagons, and collected a charge for the use of the road. Road building in America thus got its real start through private financing.

Washington was then a "little village in the midst of the woods." And the big Capitol building, just rising, looked odd standing in its half-finished state atop a muddy hill. Pennsylvania Avenue, lying between the Capitol and the White House, was in wet weather a river of mud and in dry weather so dusty that when the wind blew the dust around, near-by objects were almost invisible. Few Congressmen even considered bringing their families to the unpleasant place—they had a hard enough time of it themselves, trying to get in and out of town over the bad roads.

Harrison Gray Otis, describing the Washington-Baltimore road in 1815, in a letter to his wife wrote:

The Bladensburg Run, before we came to the bridge, was happily in no place *above* the horses' bellies. As we passed through, the driver pointed out to us the spot right under our wheels where the stage horses last year were drowned; but then he consoled us by showing the tree on which all the passengers but *one* were saved. Whether that one was gouty or not I did not inquire.

The road from Fredericksburg, Virginia, to the capitol was the "worst in the world," Thomas Jefferson had reported in 1802. It couldn't have been much improved twelve years later, for it took a Virginia congressman fifty hours to travel the same number of miles between Fredericksburg and Alexandria, a few miles from Washington.

It was during this period that the United States experienced its first invasion by European visitors. They went about the country with critical eyes, often venturing deep into the interior and gathering material for books they wrote about the people of this Republic and their peculiar customs. Captain Basil Hall of the British Royal Navy, visiting the United States in the 1820's, protested to an American friend who wanted him to take a different road through a more scenic part of his state: "Many parts we have come to are good, some are bad; these must all be jumbled together, and a fair mean taken. Besides, it is the people I want to see, and for this reason I intend going in the direction I first spoke of." And he did.

Almost all of the early tourists (if not writing books they wrote long letters home) wailed over the miserable condition of the roads. Thomas Moore, the Irish poet, was particularly upset with the Atlantic Coast roads. He wrote home:

I am now, dearest mother, more than 300 miles from Norfolk. I have passed the Potomac, the Rappahannock, the Ocoquan, and *Potapsio* and many other rivers with names as barbarous as the inhabitants. Every step I take not only *reconciles* but *endears* to me not only the excellencies but even the errors of old England. Such a road as I have come! and in such a conveyance! The mail takes twelve passengers . . . stages filled with a motley mixture "hail fellow well met," driving through mud and filth, which *bespatters* them as they *raise* it, and risking an *upset* at every step.

There were thousands of people, however, who didn't mind "risking an upset" at all. The road between Philadelphia and New York, the best in the country, was in constant use, as was the old Boston Post Road. By 1832 more than one hundred lines of coaches were operating out of Boston, bound for New York and for New England towns to the north.

Around this time a craze for speed started to spread. In spite of bad roads, stagecoach lines competed wildly in running their horses faster and faster. "We can get you there sooner," they advertised—not adding, "if we get you there alive." Travelers boasted about the speed of the coaches they rode, how little time it took them to get from place to place, as today you hear air travelers boasting, "Why only yesterday I had supper in Ireland!"

Even as far back as 1766 a stage line advertised its speed between New York and Philadelphia as a day and a half. (This time did not include that spent on a sailboat out of New York for New Jersey, in order to catch the 3:00 A. M. stage for Philadelphia.) The "coach" was no more than a springless wagon with a boxlike top, but the inspired owner, catching a vision of the speed-era that America would perhaps never outgrow, gave it a wonderful name: "The Flying Machine."

Everybody thought the speed of the gay stagecoaches the last word in traveling time. "We were rattled from Providence to Boston in four hours and fifty minutes," Seymour Dunbar quotes from a letter written in 1822. "If anyone wants to go faster he may send to Kentucky and charter a streak of lightning!"

This urge, perhaps even this craze for speed was certainly not peculiar to Americans. The early Romans, too, had liked speed and fashioned their chariots for it. The desert folk of Arabia saw not only beauty in the limbs of their Arabian horses but speed. The earliest builders of ships fashioned staunchness, first, into their vessels but shaped the hulls consciously for speed. All had their reasons and of them all Americans had the most pressing reason.

Americans had the reason of vast distances to traverse. They had, and it was felt with daily-increasing emphasis, a society and an economy where men were growing more and more dependent upon each other. The cotton-grower of Georgia found himself dependent upon the weavers of New England; the gunsmiths of New England had outlets in Kentucky. Men had to meet with men for business and politics and for simple survival, and the one able to get there first was the one who got his word in. Speed thus was a craze mainly because it was a necessity.

These early urgencies naturally left their mark upon the American character.

9. THE OTHER SIDE OF
THE MOUNTAINS

Come all of ye fine young fellows
Who have got a mind to range
Into some far off countree
Your fortune for to change.
We'll lay us down upon the banks
Of the blessed O–h–i–o;
Through the wildwoods we'll wander
And we'll chase the buffalo.

"Shoot the Buffalo"

The much-traveled coastal roads were bad; but the roads on the western side of the Alleghany Mountains were terrible. Christopher Schultz, an astonished early tourist, made a joke of them in his book, *Travels on an Inland Voyage.* "If the mud does not quite cover your boot tops when you sit in the saddle," he wrote, "they call it a middling good road."

For many years only one road crossed the Ohio. Ebenezer Zane, the pioneer who founded Wheeling, West Virginia (then in Virginia), had in 1796 blazed trees and cut away underbrush from an ancient Indian path leading from Wheeling to Limestone on the Ohio, across from Maysville, Kentucky. From there a pioneer road, marked first by buffalo, led to the lower Mississippi Valley through Kentucky and Tennessee. Only three years after the Indian trail was widened into a bridle path, United States post riders used Zane's Trace to deliver the mails—the first post route into the Northwest Territory. On Ebenezer Zane's tombstone was carved the proud statement that he was the first permanent inhabitant of that part of the "Western World."

But there were well-defined travel routes in Indiana long before Americans came to cut down trees and start farms. Paths well worn by the white man were waiting in that wilderness, paths that would one day become modern highways. For nearly two hundred years the area that is now northern Illinois had been a center for the vast French fur trade around the Great Lakes. Trails ran in all directions from the portage path where South Bend now stands, and over these trails the gay, singing French traders had wandered, making friends with the Indians and buying their furs.

For many years the only means of getting about in the Northwest Territory was on foot or on horseback. Even after the advent of crude wagon roads, in many sections all stage and wagon traffic stopped completely during the rainy season—nothing on wheels could possibly have moved over those roads. Travel between the coast and the frontier was so rugged that people spoke of it as "going into the West" or "coming out of the West." By "West," of course, they meant the land west of the Alleghenies but east of the Mississippi River, for in the early nineteenth century the great river was the edge of the last frontier.

A traveler *could* get to the border of Indiana as early as 1800 by stage wagon. Drawn by four horses, these wagons, like the early "Flying Machine," had no springs, but the bodies were much larger. Their battered passengers rode sixteen hours a day, in all weather, and over the rudest, bumpiest stump-riddled roads imaginable. What they lacked in comfort, however, the rattling wagons tried to make up in style—they were painted brilliant colors, usually gold, red, or bright blue.

Oliver H. Smith, an early pioneer to the other side of the mountains who later became a United States senator, looked back in 1858 and recalled:

At the time I came to the state [Indiana] in March, 1817, there was not a railroad in the United States, nor a canal west of the Alleghany Mountains . . . There was not a foot of turnpike road in the State and plank roads had never been heard of . . . the traveling all done on horseback, the husband mounted before on the saddle, with from one to three of the youngest children in his arms—the wife, with a spread cover reaching to the tail of the horse, sitting behind, with the balance of the children unable to walk in her lap. . . .

I stood . . . on the site of Indianapolis, the capital of our State, when there was scarcely a tree missing from the dense forest around it. I passed through the wilds of Marion on my pony, upon the winding Indian path, when the bear, the deer and the wolf sprang up before me.

Twice a month a six-ox train hauling freight made the journey between Cincinnati and Indianapolis; a post rider carried the mail in a pack-saddle.

Meanwhile, the steady drift over the mountains continued. By 1820 there were two and a half million people living on the western side of the mountains, as many people as there had been in all of the colonies before the Revolution. Each year the big covered freight wagons rumbled on for a longer distance than the year before. And always, ahead of the freight lines, were the borderers who didn't stop where the roads ended.

A traveler going "into the West" could see as he went along each distinct wave of the rolling tide from the East—if he kept going far enough. He would see the streams of emigrants leaving Kentucky, Tennessee, and North Carolina, journeying northward to find new homes in Ohio, Illinois, and Indiana. By wagon or on horseback they plugged along over rough roads to Louisville, crossed the Ohio River, and by the centuries-old path called simply Buffalo Trace made their way into Vincennes and the West.

The traveler, perhaps on an Ohio River ferry, would see thousands of other settlers from New England floating on rafts or barges down the river to their new homes. Seymour Dunbar, in *A History of Travel in America*, draws a vivid picture of the river life of the floating pioneers:

. . . quaint boats into which men, women, children, horses, pigs, chickens, cows, dogs, kegs of powder, dishes, furniture, boxes of provisions and farm implements were all loaded and jumbled together, to float down the river to somewhere . . . At night, as they drifted on the dark waters, their loopholes often spurted jets of rifle fire, while women loaded the hot rifles of the men in the flickering light of pine knots held by silent children, and watched for the answering shots of red enemies through the mist that hid them. By day, on a more kindly voyage, some backwoods genius on the cabin roof would touch the resin to his fiddle-bow and send the wild strains of a hoedown to the wooded shores and back again, while the family mule gave vent to his emotions in a loud heehaw, the pigs squealed, the children shouted and danced to the melody of the combined orchestra, and the women rolled up the bedding, milked the cow, hung out the wash and killed a few chickens for dinner.

From about 1788 until some time after the coming of steamboats to the interior rivers, an estimated million Americans made such river journeys in search of new homes, journeys lasting for week upon weary week, covering distances of a few hundred to over a thousand miles. No one, incidentally, would have called these courageous people any such high-sounding word as "pioneer." In their own time the stream of people who went westward were known simply as "the movers."

The traveler would eventually reach the growing cities of "the West." Cincinnati, central trading point for the fertile lands of Ohio and Kentucky, was the largest city in the section. St. Louis, jumping-off place for the Far West, was the fur-trading center of the upper Mississippi and Missouri rivers. By 1808 it had been incorporated as a town.

Around the cities the farms clustered close together and were cultivated in the most up-to-date methods. Farther westward, the traveler came upon scattered, small, primitive farms where whole families planted and harvested their crops in the same backbreaking way their ancestors in Europe had done for hundreds of years. They sowed by hand from bags of seed, their only implements the sickle, flail, and hoe. On all the frontier farms it was much the same, since farm machinery had not yet arrived.

Moving on, the traveler would leave the farms far behind him. Occasionally now he would see hogs rooting for acorns under huge oak trees, and cattle grazing on the wild grass. Near by might be a rude one-room log cabin, the home of a borderer who lived by his rifle and his good right arm.

At some part of the frontier our traveler would certainly have come upon one of the Army forts, and perhaps spent the night within its shelter. These posts, usually soldier-built and located on the edge of civilization, were important in the westward march of the movers. The larger posts formed a square around a parade ground, and contained officers' quarters, barracks, a hospital, quartermasters' supplies, kitchens, a laundry room, and a workshop. When the wives of young West Pointers joined their husbands at the frontier, they brought with them the gaiety of eastern coastal towns; there were "post hops" to the tune of a fast-moving fiddle, card games, and hunting parties. The forts, a protection against Indians, were frequently the scene of important treaties with them.

When our wanderer left the forts, he would be deep in the Far West. He would come upon the Indians of the great plains that stretched beyond the Mississippi, and almost certainly he would meet straggling through the wilderness the first of the American advance. These were the savagely dressed, bewhiskered fur traders who ventured deep into Indian country to obtain precious animal skins from the natives. St. Louis was as close to civilization as the fur traders ever returned.

The value of land near St. Louis and Cincinnati increased, and as the populated area grew roads began to stem out into the countryside. Farmers were able to bring their produce into the cities and for the first time make a small cash profit from their farms. So many hogs were driven along the muddy roads into Cincinnati, so much meat was packed, that the city earned the nickname "Porkopolis"!

It was seriously thought during the War of 1812 that, should the war be lost, the whole back country might fall into the possession of the British crown. In consequence many people in those changing years were afraid to risk breaking up their homes and moving their families over the mountains. But with peace came a new migration from the Atlantic

Coast and the southern states into the West. The territory of Indiana in 1810 had a population of only twenty-five thousand; when it became a state six years later, seventy thousand Hoosiers celebrated the event. Illinois was growing just as fast, and became a state in 1818. The movers were really on the move.

In 1820 the Indiana *Centinel* proudly reported:

Comfortable houses and good farms are creating on the St. Louis road, and a stage coach with passengers will soon be humming across those vast and cheerless prairies, where, but a short time since, the wolf and deer were the principal inhabitants, or men in savage attire, as ferocious and wild as they.

The area which was once the Northwest Territory remained a fur-trading center even after movers from the South and East had arrived in numbers. In 1820 Pierre Navarre, an agent for the American Fur Company, established a trading post in the old French location. Settlers in what is now northern Indiana could still see Indians paddling large canoes and piroques laden with furs along the St. Joseph River. A century later the cabin where Navarre lived with his Potawatomi Indian wife was moved from its riverbank and placed on display in Leeper Park, in South Bend, where it still stands.

In 1826 Indiana decided to do something to help the thousands of settlers moving northward through the state. It bought a strip of land from the Potawatomi Indians, sold the land to settlers, and used the money to build a road for them to travel over. This was the Michigan Road, leading north from Indianapolis through Union Town, Logansport, and South Bend. For many years it was the chief travel route between the valley of the Ohio River and Lake Michigan.

In the 1830's, with money appropriated by Congress, soldiers of the 5th Regiment of the standing army were hard at work building a road from the Mississippi River across Wisconsin, and down to Chicago. This pioneer road, connecting three Army forts, led from Prairie du Chien (Fort Crawford) through Madison northward to Fort Winnebago at Portage, and on to Fort Howard at Green Bay. It was called simply "The Military Road."

Through forest land the soldiers cut down trees for a clear track two rods wide, blazing the way by stripping off bark the size of a man's hand. Through marshes they placed logs crosswise to make a corduroy surface, and they built rude bridges wherever necessary. One of these bridges, oddly enough, was ahead of the movers; in the quiet wilderness country at Fond du Lac it had been used by Indians and wild animals until white settlers came that way.

During the building of the roadway, some soldiers from Fort Howard, apparently bored with the hard work of clearing a path, carved faces in the blazed, exposed tree trunks, and thus gave a name to that part of the route: "Mask Hill."

Many European tourists crossed the mountains to see the western country, and as usual wrote letters and books about the people, the soil and rivers, and the markets. These writings, although often accentuating the hardships, attracted many thousands of immigrants to the United States. Atlantic Ocean trading vessels were filled with hopeful passengers from England, Scotland, and Ireland—old men and women, young men and women, children and babies—bound for the United States. For most of them their "promised land" meant the cheap, fertile, wonderful country on the other side of the mountains. They bought wagons and horses if they could afford them, packed their few belongings, started out over the rough roads, and joined the ranks of American movers.

10. THE NATIONAL ROAD

It is the sincere belief of all old pike boys that the stage lines of the National Road were never equalled in spirit and dash on any road, in any age or country. The chariots of the Appian Way, drawn by the fastest horses of ancient Italy, formed a dismal cortege in comparison with the sprightly procession of stage coaches on the old American highway. The grandeur of the old mail coach is riveted forever in the memory of the pike boy. To see it ascending a long hill, increasing speed, when nearing the summit, then moving rapidly over the intervening level to the top of the next hill, and dashing down it, a driver like the stately Redding Bunting wielding the whip and handling the reins, revealed a scene that will never be forgotten.

Thomas B. Searight

This is the story of the great National Road that helped save the Union, the road of many "firsts." It was the first important road built by the United States government; it was the first good road to cut through the mountains into the West; and it was the first long road in the country (planned to run nearly seven hundred miles from the East Coast to the Mississippi River).

George Washington dreamed of such a road when he was a young man. As leader of the new country, he knew that a road *had* to be built across the great barrier formed by the Alleghenies, lest all of the West be lost to the Union. Each year the "westerners" grew more independent of the East. Many whose families had lived in the West for some time no longer had business or family links with the people of the Atlantic Coast states. Furthermore, to do any large-scale trading with New York and Baltimore, westerners had to send their produce all the way down the Mississippi and then up the Atlantic Coast. It was a dangerous situation. George Washington explored the Ohio country for himself and warned the East: "The Western States stand as it were upon a pivot."

So the National Road was built to hold the country together. George Washington did not live to see it; President Jefferson appointed the first road commissioners. The route they chose was one which buffalo and Indians centuries before had discovered as the best cut through the mountains. Starting at the Potomac River at Cumberland, Maryland, the National Road led through the Maryland and Pennsylvania country into Wheeling, Virginia, on the Ohio River. Jumping the Ohio, it continued in a splendid straight line over rolling plains through Ohio, Indiana, and Illinois. The legal name, and the early name, for this highway was "The Cumberland

Road," but after a while nearly everyone proudly called it the National Road, or "The Pike." Today it is still the most important stretch of U. S. 40.

The first section of the great National Road, built over the route of early pioneers and soldiers, was begun in 1808. Construction was stopped during the War of 1812, and it was not until 1818 that the Pike got as far as the Ohio River. The eastern part of the road already had had quite a history. In 1751, a friendly Delaware Indian named Necomolin had helped blaze this trail over the mountains for the Ohio Company, and the wilderness path was called "Necomolin's Trail" by the early pioneers who journeyed over it. It later became a military road for the British General Braddock, who widened a stretch of one hundred miles during the French and Indian War. In 1755 Braddock was killed in battle near the present city of Pittsburgh, and buried not far from the road. The burial service was read by young Lieutenant Colonel George Washington. When the war was over, west-bound pioneers took to calling Necomolin's Trail "Braddock's Road."

The building of this first super highway was one of the most fiercely debated political issues of its time. Prior to its construction, all road building had been done by individual states, but none of them could afford to build a road like the Pike; the money had to come from the United States Treasury. In Congress Henry Clay and John C. Calhoun hotly defended the road, and the government's *right* to build an interstate highway. Calhoun stated that Congress should "bind the republic together with a perfect system of roads and canals. . . . Let us conquer space. . . . It is thus that a citizen of the West will read the news of Boston still moist from the papers."

Yet even in the face of the desperate need for such a highway, Congress did not state outright that the United States government had the *power* to build roads from one state to another. Instead, when Ohio became a state in 1803, it was agreed that one-twentieth of the money made from the sale of land in the new state would be spent on roads leading from the waters of the Atlantic Ocean through Ohio. After obtaining the consent of the states through which the road passed, the United States government "advanced" the money for this road-building—and later advanced more money for the National Road, even when the sale of Ohio land failed to meet the cost of construction. The same arrangement was made with Indiana and Illinois when they became states.

President Andrew Jackson believed the government had no right to collect tolls for repair of the

National Road, and accordingly the stretch of the Pike east of the Ohio River was given back to the states in 1835. Eventually, as the years passed, the whole length of road was surrendered to the states through which it ran.

Thousands of laborers enthusiastically swarmed to this job of road building. When there was no work to be done at home, farmers living near by brought their teams of horses and pitched in, earning extra money by working on the Pike. Mostly agricultural tools were used—the ox-drawn plow broke ground; a horse-drawn scoop lifted the earth from the roadway; and wheelbarrows hauled it away.

The road was made of broken stone and gravel, and parts of it, after 1825, were "macadamized" as Mr. McAdam had ably demonstrated could be done. It was thirty feet wide in the center and cleared on each side for twenty feet, with ditches to drain off water. Large arched stone bridges which spanned the waterways were so strongly built that many are still in use today.

In August, 1818, the first stagecoach went rattling over the mountains into Wheeling. It was a great day for the country! For the first time big Conestogas could load up in Baltimore, easily follow a good Pike through Frederick, Hagerstown, and Cumberland, get on the National Road and continue over the mountains to the Ohio River. At first the only way of crossing the Ohio was by ferry; but finally a great bridge was built.

Beyond this point, however, the National Road crawled westward very slowly. The last section was not completed until 1852—and it never got quite as far west as Vandalia, Illinois, except on a survey. But as soon as a section of the Pike was opened, it was used immediately by road-hungry people. During the period when the National Road was the only wagon road for west-bound emigrants, the combined population of Illinois, Indiana, and Ohio jumped from 783,635 to 3,620,314.

Traffic went both ways. Stagecoaches carrying mail and newspapers as well as passengers, Conestoga wagons loaded with tons of freight, smaller covered wagons hauling whole families and their belongings, pack-horse caravans, farmers driving hogs, sheep, and cattle to market—all swarmed on the Pike. Much of the goods formerly floated down the Mississippi River to New Orleans now rode eastward in the big wagons.

By 1830 a stagecoach was an elegant sight, the outside handsomely painted in bright colors, the interior lined with silk plush. The body, swung on wide leather straps, had three seats which held nine passengers comfortably. Painted on both doors of the coach was its name—there were coaches named for nearly every state and big city in this country, some for foreign countries, and for national heroes. Farmers working in fields by the National Road stopped work, leaned on their plows, and marveled at the speed and elegance of the coaches flashing by: the *Pocahontas, Columbus, Washington,* and the *Henry Clay;* the *Sultana, Ivanhoe,* and—*Erin Go Bragh!*

Several big stage companies and many smaller lines on the National Pike competed bitterly to carry the mails and passengers. And *every* stage line struggled for speed and more speed. "Make this time or we will find someone who will," they printed on notices to drivers. Rhymes, couplets, and amusing little jingles arose from this rivalry, most of them based on the assumption that no passenger wanted to be "passed." Thus:

If you take a seat on Stockton's line
You are sure to be passed by Pete Burdine.

Pete Burdine was one of the well-known stage drivers. Another was booming-voiced Redding Bunting who stood six and a half feet tall. Once he drove his big mail stage 131 miles in twelve hours, carrying President Polk's message that the United States was at war with Mexico.

There was steady, noisy, constant movement on the National Road. Thomas B. Searight, who grew up on the Pike, wrote:

> As many as twenty-four horse coaches have been counted in line at one time on the road, and large, broad-wheeled wagons covered with white canvas stretched over bows laden with merchandise and drawn by six Conestoga horses were visible all day long at every point, and many times until late in the evening, besides innumerable caravans of horses, mules, cattle, hogs and sheep. It looked more like a leading avenue of a great city than a road through rural districts. . . .

Situated every mile or so along the Pike were wagonhouses for the drivers of the big Conestoga freighters, with large yards for the horses who slept in the open beside the heavy loads they pulled all day. In summertime the wagoners slept in the open too; but on cold winter nights they stretched out on the floor of the wagonhouse, wrapped in their own blankets. The term stogy is supposed to have been derived from the wagoners, who were all avid smokers. One alert manufacturer made long cigars out of low-grade tobacco, designed especially for the wagoners. These sold four-for-a-cent and were so cheap they didn't have a name! For that reason they were called "Conestogas"—then "Conestogys"—then finally, as even today—"stogies."

Andrew Jackson passed in splendid triumph over parts of the National Road, as did Presidents Monroe, Harrison, Polk, and Tyler. They were popular heroes. President Van Buren, who also traveled over the road, was not—for he opposed the extension of the Pike. Once Henry Clay had an upset in a coach on the road; he brushed off his clothes and remarked that the Clay of Kentucky was now mixed with the limestone of Pennsylvania.

The National Road was the chief means of transportation from the Atlantic Ocean to the Mississippi River from 1817 until about the middle of the century, but a road-building boom was in progress all over the settled parts of the country. By 1830 there were twenty-seven thousand miles of surfaced roads, most of them turnpikes stemming out from larger towns. Five years later a steam shovel was patented, and with this invention to lighten the backbreaking labor of road-building, the future of highways looked very bright indeed.

However, as the National Road approached the Mississippi, other means of transportation caught the national favor: the whole country became wildly enthusiastic about canals and railroads, and for a while many people thought there was no future for "common" roads at all! Where railroads didn't go, they argued, canals would.

Nearly a hundred years of American history were to pass before citizens effected the second road-building boom.

11. New York's Big Ditch:
THE ERIE CANAL

And there's the state of New York
Where some are very rich,
Themselves and a few others
Have dug a mighty ditch
To render it more easy
For us to find the way
To sail upon the waters
To Michigania,
Yea, yea, yea—to Michigania!

Chantey of Erie Canal travelers

For a period of about thirty years, beginning in 1817, America had its great day of canals.
They sprang into the American transportation scene
with almost startling abruptness, and canal construction proceeded with feverish haste; during this
short time more than four thousand miles were
built. George Washington, years before the "big
ditches" came, had dreamed of a vast network of
canals uniting each section of the country. His
dreams—and some of his plans—became real.

Benjamin Franklin, also ahead of his time, had
seen the practicality of canals. In 1770 he wrote

from England to the mayor of Philadelphia concerning a canal to join the Schuylkill and Susquehanna rivers: "Rivers are ungovernable things, especially in hilly countries. Canals are quiet and always manageable . . . I warmly wish success to every Attempt for Improvement of our dear Country."

The canals helped build the country, as our first President had known they would, for from the waters of these canals were spawned many of the thriving cities in the region of the Great Lakes.

The Erie Canal, most important of them all, was New York's answer to the National Road. "Come to Philadelphia!" the Lancaster Pike had said, and mountain pack horses met the Conestogas, exchanging goods, helping Pennsylvania grow rich and powerful. "Bring your trade to the East this way," said the National Pike, and big freight wagons lumbered into Baltimore and the growing southern cities with the products of the western country. "Now come to New York!" the Erie Canal shouted to prized trade on the other side of the mountains. And the Erie Canal, New York's wonderful water-road, settled the question.

Francis P. Kimball, in *New York—the Canal State*, says of this turn of the wheel:

The effects of the Erie Canal swept mightily through New York from the Lakes to seaboard.

. . .Land values rose $100,000,000 in five years.
The state, which had been fourth in population in
1800, became first in 1820, and held that position
undisputed thereafter. Up to that time, New York
had been slower than Pennsylvania in its development. Philadelphia's exports in 1795 were forty
per cent more than those of New York; in 1825,
were forty-five per cent less. New Orleans, having
the Mississippi at its back, was really predicted for
America's premier port. . . . But the Erie Canal
gradually turned the balance-wheel to the East.
. . .Thus, in a few brief years, New York had
been lifted out of a primitive and disorganized
condition into a thriving, unified and growing
commonwealth.

It took years of political scheming to draw up the
plans for the Erie Canal, for to most people of the
time the project seemed fantastic. To dig a canal
through hundreds of miles of wilderness and swamps
seemed as improbable as drilling a hole through the
center of the earth to China. Three hundred and
sixty miles west of Albany is Buffalo, built on the
waters of Lake Erie. The land route between Albany
and Buffalo, in the old days an Indian portage path,
became the route of the Erie Canal. It linked the
fresh waters of Lake Erie with the salt water of the
Atlantic Ocean by way of the Hudson River, and it

served the same main purpose as the National Road—
it brought two sections of the country closer together.

New York State financed its canal at a cost of seven
million dollars. It was then the largest state construction job ever executed, and perhaps the strang-
est. De Witt Clinton, Governor of New York,
shrewdly ordered work on the canal started in the
middle, at Rome, where the going was easiest, so
there would be less chance for politicians to halt
construction.

On the Fourth of July, 1817, digging began.
Workmen took machinery never thought of before
into the forests and swamps to cut down the
centuries-old trees, and dig the canal through western New York State. During the winter they hauled
in provisions and equipment by sled over the snow-
covered ground—this was easier than struggling with
heavy supplies over forest trails. By the next year
there were two thousand men working on the Erie
Canal, and two thousand straining horses and oxen
pulling at the heavy plows and scrapers. In July,
1823, the part of the canal between Schenectady
and Rome was completed and in use.

The workmen clawed slowly through the dense
forests. When they reached the hot swamplands
they worked almost naked. A swamp sickness they
called "canal fever" crept in and many men died—
construction was once halted altogether for several

weeks while the sick laborers recovered from their plague. But the work went on and the canal was finished. There it was—forty feet wide, four feet deep, 360 miles long, with eighty-two locks overcoming a difference in water levels of nearly six hundred feet. It had taken eight years to dig the "big ditch," and it had been built entirely by rule-of-thumb by engineers who had no blueprints to guide them.

In October, 1825, the first boat to be towed across the canal, the *Seneca Chief*, carried kegs of water from Lake Erie to be dumped into the Atlantic. A cannon was fired in Buffalo as the canal procession left town; and when the sound was heard at the next relay point along the canal, another cannon was fired; and so along the entire length of the big ditch. Eighty-one minutes later, excited citizens in New York heard the cannon nearest them, and they knew that their Erie Canal was finally in operation. When the *Seneca Chief* pulled into New York Harbor three and a half days later, the town went wild with speeches, dances, fireworks, and a big parade to celebrate the canal opening. Miffed Philadelphians called the merrymaking a "Roman holiday."

It was much cheaper to ship freight by canal than by Conestoga wagon. Soon businessmen from Baltimore and Philadelphia were sending goods along the Atlantic Coast, up the Hudson River to Albany, and then by the Erie Canal to Buffalo and Lake Erie.

The Erie Canal was planned by politicians and businessmen as a means of hauling freight; it hadn't occurred to them that Americans, who are usually several jumps ahead of their freight lines, would leap at the chance to travel westward by canal. But people with itching feet immediately saw the Erie Canal as a westward water-road for themselves—and a new kind of business came to the canal. Special boats were built for passengers, divided into two kinds. One was the fast-moving canal packet, with sleeping and eating arrangements; the other was the slower line boat, which cost less to ride. People leaving their homes behind them for new homes in the West used the latter type. The stream of movers had found another way to move.

Canal barges and boats were pulled by horses or mules walking ahead along the towpath; the one attempt at using steam was an unsuccessful experiment.

Canal "packets," named for the fast sailboats that plowed the Atlantic Coast, were about eighty feet long, eight feet high, and eleven feet wide. Trips in them were no luxury cruises. The packets usually had two large rooms, one for men and one for women and children. In the early evening, with the passengers reading, writing letters, and smoking, the rooms were lounges. At night the captain and his two helpers brought in wooden slabs and the rooms became bedrooms. They attached the slabs to the wall in tiers three-deep, threw lumpy straw mattresses on them—and the beds were ready. Since sleeping space was seldom assigned, the beds were grabbed on a first-come-first-served basis. The hindmost, if the boat was crowded, slept on mattresses thrown on the floor. If floor space was limited, they slept on tables *over* the people on the floor!

Charles Dickens once made a trip on a canal packet, which he described in *American Notes*. He was particularly displeased with the sleeping arrangements:

I have mentioned my having been in some uncertainty and doubt, at first, relative to the sleeping arrangements on board this boat. I remained in the same vague state of mind until ten o'clock or thereabouts, when going below, I found suspended on either side of the cabin, three long tiers of hanging book-shelves, designed apparently for volumes of the small octavo size. Looking with greater attention at these contrivances (wondering to find such literary preparations in such a place), I descried on each shelf a sort of microscopic sheet and blanket; then I began dimly to comprehend that the passengers were the library, and that they were to be arranged, edge-wise, on these shelves, till morning.

. . . I was at first in some uncertainty as to the

best means of getting into it. But the shelf being a bottom one, I finally determined on lying upon the floor, rolling gently in, stopping immediately I touched the mattress, and remaining for the night with that side uppermost, whatever it might be. Luckily, I came upon my back at exactly the right moment.

. . . One of two remarkable circumstances is indisputably a fact, with reference to that class of society who travel in these boats. Either they carry their restlessness to such a pitch that they never sleep at all, or they expectorate in dreams. . . . All night long, and every night, on this canal, there was a perfect storm and tempest of spitting . . .

At night a line was strung around the room for the passengers to hang their clothes on. For washing purposes, they dropped a bucket overboard and dipped up water from the canal. A comb and hairbrush, for common use, were chained to the wall near a mirror. During the day passengers played cards and games, read or wrote letters in the main room, or sat high on the flat topdeck admiring the view, watching the horses or mules as they trudged on ahead. However, even during the day the trip had its discomforts. Where a road crossed the canal and the bridge was low, all the people on deck sprawled flat across the deck to keep from being scraped off when the captain shouted "Low bridge!"

As a rule the line boats did not offer beds and meals, but their passengers didn't mind the slower rate of travel, nor did they care to spend more money for the convenience of packet travel on the canal. The movers knew where they were going, and they knew that by the canal they could get deep into the uncut forests around the Great Lakes. To them time was not as important as saving money.

Many of the movers had been moving for some time, for they had crossed the Atlantic Ocean. When the Erie Canal was opened in 1825 there were only about eight thousand immigrants a year; by 1830 more than fifty thousand people were coming into the United States annually. Many of these new people preferred to go into the West where land was selling for a dollar and a quarter an acre, and a man could be truly independent. Those who wanted to settle in southern Ohio, Indiana, and Illinois often traveled by the National Road, while others who dared the less populated region around the Great Lakes used the Erie Canal. The canal became a new kind of highway for thousands of people, both native Americans and the Europeans who would soon become Americans.

The region which was the West, and which is now the central part of the country, grew rapidly as a result of the Erie Canal. In 1810, only fifteen years before the canal was built, Ohio was the thirteenth state in population. By 1840, because of the canal and the National Road, it had grown to be the third largest. Before the canal came, there were only a few settlements in Michigan and Wisconsin. The northern sections of Illinois, Indiana, and Ohio were vast stretches of uncut forests. The only roads connecting the few settlements were rutted, miry, and cluttered with tree stumps; over these the few settlers had to haul their products to water and set them afloat downstream on barges and flatboats. But with the coming of the canal the whole area bordering the Great Lakes changed. Lake Erie, now connected by water with the entire world, became a great trade route. Thousands of vessels came into port at Buffalo laden with western wheat, lumber, and often furs, which were sent on to New York. The same vessels left Buffalo loaded down again, this time with movers who crossed the lake and settled inland. Shipping on the Great Lakes increased, and Chicago grew from a village in 1835 to a city of twenty-five thousand by 1847.

Other canals were constructed. Lake Champlain, lying between Vermont and upper New York State, was connected by canal with Lake Ontario, and this in turn with Lake Erie. Eventually all the Great Lakes were joined by canals, and the enormous products of the region could be moved by boat the entire distance over the lakes to Buffalo, where they were transferred to barges on the Erie Canal, and thence down the Hudson River straight into New York City.

The big ditch which had been so ridiculed was a magnificent success. Within ten years the state of New York, which had paid seven million dollars for the Erie Canal, got its money back in toll charges. What New York City gained is inestimable.

Immediately the whole country became canal-conscious, and almost feverishly more ditches were dug. Many people, long after Washington was dead, agreed with him in believing that canals would forever take the place of roads for both freight and passenger travel. The Chesapeake and Ohio Canal, planned by Washington many years before, connected the Potomac River at Washington with Cumberland, Maryland. Begun in 1828, it was finished, after many delays and arguments, in 1850. The C & O Canal never got any farther than Cumberland, although it was planned to join the Ohio River at Pittsburgh.

Ohio spent sixteen million dollars on canal building, and Indiana constructed 379 miles of canals costing six million dollars. Illinois, Pennsylvania, Maryland, and New Jersey caught the canal fever, and began digging. South Carolina already had its Santee Canal into Charleston, and New Orleans had its Carondelet Canal connecting it with the Gulf of Mexico.

But the times of the man-made water roads had to end, for whenever a faster method to travel and to move freight is found, Americans are quick to discard the old. Pack-horse caravans served well for trade with the borderers in colonial times, but they were replaced by Conestoga wagons. Flatboats drifting down the Mississippi River had their brief years until steamboats took their place. So it was with canals. Railroad tracks were stretching farther and farther west toward the Mississippi, and there came a time when trains replaced most of the canal barges and packets.

12. THE IRON HORSE

Oh, it's once I made money by driving a team
But now all is hauled on the railroad by steam.
May the devil catch the man that's invented the plan
For it's ruined us poor wagoners and every other man.

Now all you jolly wagoners, who have got good wives,
Go home to your farms and there spend your lives.
When your corn is all cribbed and your small grain is sowed,
You will have nothing to do but curse the railroad.

Song of the wagoners

By 1825 there was a railroad in England which carried people as well as coal. At this time the United States was at the beginning of its great industrial growth. Fleets of steamboats moved up and down the Mississippi River, the Erie Canal was open for business, and the great National Road pushed on into the West. Thousands of miles away from this buzzing eastern activity, Santa Fe traders were quietly opening up the Far West.

These were things that people could understand; the new kind of road in England was not. The railroad was strange and foreign-seeming to most Americans. Few people showed any enthusiasm at all, and no one foresaw the tremendous change the railroad would make in American life. Nevertheless, Americans experimented with railroads, too.

On the Fourth of July in 1828, an old man of ninety years bent down and proudly spaded over a handful of earth, the beginning of the Baltimore & Ohio's track. On the Fourth of July fifty years before, this same man, Charles Carroll, had signed the Declaration of Independence. Now the only man alive who had signed that document, he looked at the earth he had dug up for the railroad and remarked that what he had done was second in importance "only to signing the Declaration of Independence, if even second to that." The B & O line, running thirteen miles to Ellicott's Mills from Baltimore, was opened in May, 1830.

For nearly three years the railroad men didn't know whether the cars would be pulled over the tracks by horses or by steam engine. They experimented constantly—once they put a horse on top of a treadmill platform; another time they rigged up a basketlike car with sails, so that the wind could blow it along the tracks. This didn't work because the wind would not always co-operate in blowing the sailing car in the scheduled direction. Finally a contrary wind blew the whole top rigging "overboard," and this experiment was abandoned.

In 1830 Peter Cooper built a small steam locomotive for the B & O which he called the *Tom*

Thumb, and which some other amused people called a "teakettle on a truck." It could go four miles an hour and pull a car carrying twenty-four people. In August of that year the *Tom Thumb* was challenged to race a horse. The horse won the race because a belt on the locomotive slipped, and for a year or more horses were used to pull the wagons on the B & O.

South Carolina's Charleston & Hamburg Railroad began operation in January, 1831, with its first American-made locomotive, called *The Best Friend of Charleston.* It brought into the port of Charleston bales of cotton which once were shipped from inland Georgia to the port of Savannah. Business in Charleston boomed. The *Best Friend* worked until its fireman, tired of hearing the constant hissing noise from the safety valve, sat down on the valve. The restless steam, seeking escape and finding none, blew the engine up—and that was the end of the *Best Friend.* A new locomotive, the *West Point,* was obtained and it pulled its car over what was then the longest railroad in the world—135 miles.

Other iron horses came to replace the real horses that pulled stages, wagons, and canal boats: the Philadelphia, Germantown and Morristown Railroad in Pennsylvania; the Mohawk and Hudson in New York; the Camden and Amboy Railroad in New Jersey. Most trains, recalling the accident to the *Best Friend,* ran a special car called a "barrier" between the locomotive and passenger cars. It was loaded with bales of cotton to keep flying sparks away from the passengers, and also to catch the engine in case it blew up.

The first railroad passenger cars resembled stage-coaches in design; but they had no springs, no cushions, and no glass in the doors or the windows. They were fastened together by chains. When the train started, the chains jerked and the passengers' heads jerked back. When it stopped, they were pitched violently forward. Engineers took up the fares, putting a chalk mark on hats to show the fare had been paid. There were no regular schedules at all. One advertisement simply stated that the trains would run "three times each day during the warm season, and twice a day during the cold season, ex-cepting Sundays." Later, when the trains ran more often, coal stoves were used to heat the cars.

At first trains ran only in the daytime. When they began hauling freight at night, they used candle lanterns with reflectors as powerful as could be made. An engineer on a southern line had his locomotive push the headlight. This was a small car with sand on its floor, and over the sand a bright pine-knot bonfire burned, lighting the track ahead. The locomotive it-self kept the glare from the engineer's eyes.

Cordwood for fuel was piled at intervals along the track on some lines, and the engineer stopped and loaded on the amount needed when the train's supply ran low. Some trains carried leather buckets swung from hooks at the side of the tank. When water was needed, the trainman stopped again at a convenient stream or river, and lowered the buckets for water. This practice led to the expression "jerk-water railroads."

At the beginning most people objected to the railroads, probably because they were afraid of them. Farmers particularly took a dim view of the iron horse, thinking that some day railroads would end forever the building of turnpikes and canals, and thus cut them off from their distant markets. Farmers near the tracks complained that the smoke would kill their poultry, and the locomotives would kill their stray cows. Railroad men simply went on building and extending their lines; but they did invent a "cow-catcher."

During the 1830's and 1840's there was a great deal of public discussion as to which kind of road was best: the railroad, the canal—or water-road—or the turnpike road. New England farmers sat around fat stoves in country stores and debated the question. Southern merchants and planters met their friends and neighbors in the county courthouse yard, hitched up their horses, and argued about railroads, canals, and turnpikes. In the fast-growing "western" states the question was vital. Politicians, canvassing their districts, tried to win votes by arguing their own stand regarding railroads. Some were for them, of course, and some against.

Pennsylvania, never to be outdone in the race for roads of whatever kind, tried a combination on the route between Philadelphia and Pittsburgh. The Main Line Railroad ran from Philadelphia to a place near Harrisburg, where it connected with a canal leading to the foot of the mountains at Hollidaysburg. Here an astonishing arrangement called the Portage Railroad continued the route. The canal boats were pulled up the mountains over inclined planes by ropes attached to a stationary engine at the top, and then lowered on the western side to Johnstown. Special railway carriages carried the canal passengers over the mountain. That is how Pennsylvania, unable to dig a canal through the mountains, climbed over them with a railroad for canal boats. It seems crazy; but it worked.

Charles Dickens made this canal-railroad trip, and said of the mountain passage:

Occasionally the rails are laid upon the extreme verge of a giddy precipice; and looking from the carriage window the traveler gazes sheer down without a stone or scrap of fence between, into the mountain depths below. The journey is very carefully made, however, only two carriages traveling together; and while proper precautions are taken it is not to be dreaded for its dangers.

There were dangers on the early railroads, of course, before the days of telegraph and double tracks. But in spite of "concussions," as collisions were then called, and other accidents, the railroads kept right on building. They improved passenger coaches and freight cars, methods of signaling, tracks, and headlights, and with each improvement became safer and more comfortable.

By 1850 there were more than nine thousand miles of track in the United States, running north and south, east and west. Six years later the Atlantic Ocean and the Mississippi River were linked by railroad. A few people dared to think that one day it might be possible to travel across the continent by railroad.

The United States needed these steam highways—but during the years of rapid railroad building, little was done to keep wagon roads in repair. Steadily they grew worse and worse. That was the beginning of what has been called the "dark ages of the roads." Stagecoach companies saw their passengers changing over to the railroads, and Conestoga freight companies saw their former trade transferred to railroad freight cars. Many lines went bankrupt. Coaches and wagons were put up for sale at auction, and a great number of them were hauled across the Mississippi River for use in the West, where in spite of trains they were used for many years.

One hundred years earlier pack-horse men had been bitter against the drivers of the Conestoga wagons, who were replacing them. Now it was the turn of the wagoners to see their own jobs disappearing, their method of hauling freight becoming clumsy, and they viewed the change with equal bitterness.

THE WESTWARD TREK

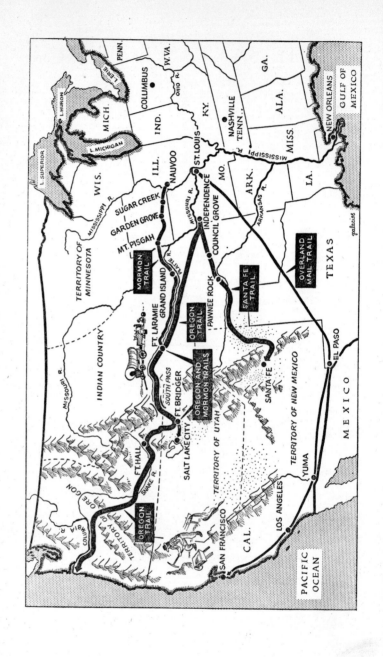

13. THE SANTA FE TRAIL

Valley, range, and high trail, mesa, butte and river
Sun across the lowlands, rolling down to rest:
There'll always be the skyline, running on forever,
Running on forever, down the long road West.
                              Henry Herbert Knibbs

Let us pause now and look back to see what was happening in the wide, lonely lands beyond the Mississippi. Thirty years before the first locomotive puffed its steam against the river barrier, daring traders had "jumped off" into the Far West to pound out with tired feet and tumbling wagon wheels the long and dangerous Santa Fe Trail.

Nearly a thousand miles southwest from the frontier fur-trading town of St. Louis was New Mexico, a mysterious and foreign country. Entry into this land was forbidden to Americans, and only a few explorers and traders had risked their lives to go there. Those who came back told stories of the long, hard journey, of fierce Indians hidden in mountain passes, of the hot desert, and of the country's capital, Santa Fe. But they spoke also of Spanish-bred mules and horses, bright Indian blankets, silver-trimmed saddles, and the clinking coins that might one day be currency for American goods.

The time came when the people of New Mexico grew tired of Spanish rule. There was a revolution, and the Spanish ruling class was overthrown. New officials took over the government, and Missouri traders began to think again of Santa Fe.

One trader in Franklin, Missouri, made plans to go there. On the first day of September, 1821, William Becknell struck out for Santa Fe with a small band of men and loaded pack horses. Somehow they made the long journey over the southwestern plains, craggy mountains, and canyon passes. Becknell was graciously received by the Governor, who asked many questions about Americans and their towns, welcomed American trade, and invited settlers to come to New Mexico.

When Becknell and his party returned home in December, they dumped their rawhide packages on the sidewalks of Franklin. Excited bystanders watched one of the men cut the thongs, and they saw the shining silver dollars spill out, clinking over the stone pavement into the gutter. The Santa Fe trade had begun. The next year Becknell went back to Santa Fe with his pack horses burdened with American goods. This time he led the animals away from the mountains and across the plains. The route he chose became the Santa Fe Trail, the first overland roadway to the Far West.

In only two years the patient pack horses were replaced by covered wagons pulled by oxen, and Becknell's trail became a wagon road. The wagons themselves, once made in Pittsburgh for the long haul westward, were soon replaced by "Murphy wagons" made in St. Louis and named after their builder. They were given the affectionate name "prairie schooners" because in the tall waving grass, with only their white canvas tops showing, they looked rather like ships plowing through a brown-green sea.

By 1828, two hundred men were making their way over the trail, carrying goods costing 150,000 dollars in the United States. Independence, Missouri, became the jumping-off place. It was a wild, restless, stirring town then, the last place where wagons could be mended, animals shod, and provisions bought for those planning to "hit the trail." Traders, Indians, Mexicans, gentlemen in beaver hats, rivermen—American "alligator-horses" and French-Canadian *voyageurs*—gamblers, wagoners driving big Conestogas in from the East, Murphies loading up for the West, all gathered at Independence.

The prairie schooners rolled out of Independence toward Santa Fe loaded with guns and ammunition, with utensils, and with materials and ornaments for the Spanish señoritas: bolts of fast-color calico, velvets, ribbons, and gay plaid shawls. The goods might be worth a thousand dollars or more, each wagon another thousand dollars. Ten days away at a wooded place called Council Grove the covered wagons met to form a caravan, and last-minute preparations were made. The men greased their wagon wheels, mended harnesses, and cut down hickory trees. The stout hickory logs would be needed in case of wagon breakdowns, for only soft cottonwood grew farther on.

From Council Grove the prairie schooners lumbered out into the Southwest, one hundred wagons, two hundred men, eight hundred animals—mules and oxen—rising and dipping over the rolling prairie. For nearly one thousand miles they faced danger from Indians and from treacherous stretches of the trail. Ahead of them was the hot desert to cross before they reached the foreign country. Far away were the smokestacks of eastern cities, the fine brick houses with their prim curtains, towns with tree-shaded sidewalks, and the sound of church bells on Sunday.

At first they traveled four abreast for better protection. They made, on an average, seventeen miles a day, stopping for a midday meal which they called "nooning it." Food generally was beans and bacon, but farther down the trail buffalo furnished fresh meat. At night a "corral," or horseshoe circle, was formed by the wagons. After the animals grazed, the men brought them inside the corral and hung an iron chain across the opening. A watch was always posted at night.

The going grew more difficult about a week away from Council Grove. Water became hard to find, and at some streams there was quicksand which could suck under a man or horse. The pioneers stuck big sticks into the sand; if this test showed quicksand they crossed the stream at a different place. At the ford finally chosen heavy branches were placed over the water, and piled high with grass and twigs. Then, in a rush, the heavy wagons were driven over the crude bridge.

Pawnee Rock at the Arkansas River was a landmark on the Santa Fe Trail. Here a member of the caravan would ride up to the highest ridge to watch for Indians who might suddenly attack while the wagon train crossed the stream. There had been little danger from Indians during the pack-horse days on the trail, and even for some years after the covered wagons came; but for four long years, beginning in 1828, the Comanches raided constantly.

After the Cimarron crossing, miles beyond Pawnee Rock, the caravans usually rested a while. The men built campfires and baked an extra supply of bread and meat. Each man filled his five-gallon water jug, and the animals drank their fill. Here there were two possible routes: one ran westward through the mountains, the other crossed the Arkansas and the sand hills on the other side, following from there a route southwestward over the Cimarron desert. The desert route, though seventy-five miles shorter, was much more dangerous. If it rained on the desert, the animals went crazy with the smell of water, often stampeding and turning over the heavy wagons. If it didn't rain, and water supplies ran low, the men had to dig deep into the sand to find water for themselves and their animals.

At a point called Ocate Creek the mountain and desert routes came together for the final push of 144 miles into Santa Fe. For the last fifty miles of the long trip the wagon voyagers filed past the lonely ruins of Pecos Pueblo, with its marvelous view of the New Mexican land and distant mountains. They went through the Glorieta Pass and on to the final high ridge. Now at last they could see the town of Santa Fe. In excitement the men threw their hats into the air, or stood in their stirrups and rose high above their horses, shouting and yelling in happiness. Even the animals caught the mood of excitement, pricked their ears, and pranced through the muddy lanes of the town. The Spaniards welcomed them as heroes, shouting loudly *"Los Americanos! La entrada de la caravana!"* The men in their tinseled, embroidered jackets waved wide sombreros in gay salute, and the señoritas smiled and waved, their bright red skirts and shawls a splash of color against the whitewashed adobe houses.

Some traders rented small stores facing the town plaza, and marketed their wares directly to the people. Others, in more of a hurry, sold their wagonloads in lump to Santa Fe storekeepers. At night there was card playing and music, and the *Yanqui* boys learned to dance the fandango with the Spanish girls.

Trade over the Santa Fe Trail grew rapidly. To protect American lives and property, President Andrew Jackson ordered soldiers to convoy the covered wagons as far as the resting place on the Arkansas River. On the way back the New Mexican government provided an escort to the point where American soldiers waited for the return trip. In 1843, when trade was at its peak, nearly a half-million dollars in American goods were hauled over the long trail.

The trail helped to shape the faces and characters of the men who rode over it, but it did more than that. It opened a way into the Far West, beckoning still more people across the wide Missouri to help build the new country for America.

The United States' war with Mexico came quickly and ended quickly; by 1848 it was all over. Santa Fe had been one of the first cities seized by American troops. Two years later the United States government owned by treaty all the land of the great southwest—California, Nevada, Utah, Colorado, Arizona, New Mexico. After the war, trade with Santa Fe was renewed, and once more oxen and mules pulled over the trail their heavy burdens of American goods to be exchanged for bright silver dollars.

14. A Half Million Movers:
THE OREGON TRAIL

Their long chained lines of yoked and patient steers;
Their long white trains that pointed to the west,
Beyond the savage west; the hopes and fears
Of blunt, untutored men, who hardly guessed
Their course; the brave and silent women, dressed
In homely spun attire, the boys in bands,
The cheery babes that laughed at all, and blessed
The doubting hearts, with laughing lifted hands! . . .
What exodus for far untraversed lands!

Joaquin Miller

While adventurers and traders were traveling the southern route, families of earnest Americans were moving northwest along an incredible road that they built as they went. They were going to the Oregon country.

Fur traders were the first white men to hear of, and then to see, the new land, and their tales of that wonderful far country spread through frontier towns, and slowly back East. They said that everything a farmer could want was there: rich soil, rivers for water power, enormous trees for homes and fuel. And there was food for the taking, salmon in the rivers, game in the forests. But the Oregon country was two thousand roadless miles beyond the frontier of the 1830's.

Then came the Panic of 1837. It struck disastrously; in this as in every depression, restlessness and discontent crept over the land. The Oregon country—where good earth was free—sounded like the answer to a lot of people's problems: to men in New England milltowns, out of jobs, out of luck; to small farmers in Mississippi and Alabama, squeezed tight by a spreading plantation system; to the men of frontier towns in what is now the Middle West, unused to hard times.

In the fall of 1843 a small band of 875 people struggled into Oregon. It was a struggle not only for them, the first to strike out, but also for the band of one thousand who followed the next year. Yet people refused to be defeated by the hardships, and in 1845 three thousand more made their way to the Oregon country. Every year new groups poured over the long trail—a half-million people, altogether! In 1852, at one point, an unbroken line of wagons stretched for five hundred miles, with other long caravans a few hundred miles ahead—and more wagon trains forming far behind.

Every wagon that made the trek eased the way a little for the wagon behind, and the wheels of these half-million people packed down the earth for more than two thousand miles from the Mississippi River to the Pacific Ocean. The road as it finally grew was one hundred feet wide, swelling in some places to ten to twenty miles wide! This was the Oregon Trail. For the most part, it was a trunkline of famous Indian trails. Fort Laramie and Fort Bridger in Wyoming and Fort Hall in Idaho, primarily trading posts rather than forts, were important stopping points along the way.

As its start, for a two-day journey of forty miles, the trail followed the Santa Fe Trail from Independence to a crossroad where a crude sign pointed: "Road to Oregon." From there it led across the plains, following the south bank of Platte River, cut through the Rocky Mountains at the famous South Pass in Wyoming, following the Green and Snake rivers to Immigrants Pass, and down the Columbia River. There many of the movers placed their wagons on rafts and poled themselves along the river into the Willamette Valley. Others, preferring to travel by land, stayed on the river road.

In the early days of the trail, both Great Britain and the United States claimed the Oregon territory—thus the early movers to the rich "nobody's land" held their acres by squatters' rights. Even while the first band of movers was rolling over the plains, this comment appeared in the Edinburgh *Review*:

However the political questions between England and America, as to the ownership of Oregon, may be decided, Oregon will never be colonized overland from the United States. The world must assume a new face before the American wagons may trace a road to the Columbia as they have done to the Ohio.

Most Englishmen believed this. They had no way of knowing that American wagons were already tracing a road; that the part of America known then as the "Western World" *was* assuming a new face. The old days of "mountain men" and fur traders were ending; the new day of permanent settlement in the Far West was just begun. Back East, Horace Greeley loudly urged the youth of the U.S.A. to "Go West, young man!" These words were the catchphrase of the times, and the young men—and the middle-aged and their wives and children, too—went.

It was a long, rough journey, hard for people and harder for horses and oxen pulling heavy wagons mile after mile, day after day. Thousands arrived at the end of the trail minus the treasured possessions they had started out with. What good was a fine old mahogany table if exhausted oxen threatened to die pulling it? One by one the parlor table, the cast-iron stoves, beds, feather mattresses, and household equipment would be thrown off the wagon. Often they were neatly stacked for luckier families farther back, with a neighborly sign: "Help yourself." The trail was littered with pathetic bits of household goods as well as with bleaching buffalo bones, and with the carcasses of horses and oxen.

Francis Parkman, in *The Oregon Trail,* describes a caravan of early movers:

. . . we saw close before us the emigrant caravan, with its heavy white wagons creeping on in slow procession and a large drove of cattle following behind. Half a dozen yellow-visaged Missourians, mounted on horseback, were cursing and shouting among them, their lank angular proportion enveloped in brown homespun, evidently cut and adjusted by the hands of a domestic female tailor. As we approached they called out to us: "How are ye, boys? Are ye for Oregon or California?"

As we pushed rapidly by the wagons, childrens' faces were thrust out from the white coverings to look at us; while the careworn, thin-featured matron, or the buxom girl, seated in front, suspended the knitting on which most of them were engaged to stare at us with wondering curiosity. By the side of each wagon stalked the proprietor, urging on his patient oxen who shouldered heavily along, inch by inch, on their interminable journey. It was easy to see that fear and dissension prevailed among them; some of the men—but these, with one exception, were bachelors—looked wistfully upon us as we rode lightly and swiftly by, and then impatiently at their own lumbering wagons and heavy-gaited oxen. Others were unwilling to advance at all until the party they had left behind should have rejoined them. Many were murmuring against the leader they had chosen, and wished to depose him; and this discontent was fomented by some ambitious spirits who had hopes of succeeding in his place. The women were divided between regrets for the homes they had left and fear of the deserts and savages before them.

The Indians, who perhaps thought of the white fur traders as being wayfarers from tribes similar to their own, were completely awed by the onrush of hundreds of thousands of people in "wheeled tepees." Worried and bewildered by this strange invasion over what they called "Big Medicine Road," the Indians nonetheless stole everything they could get their hands on. Some settlers were killed in these scrimmages, but in the early years there was little real trouble from Indians. It was not until the sixties that the tribes realized the newcomers were fast killing off the buffalo, on which they depended for food. Then the bitterness of the western tribes burst into violence.

Many movers who foolishly left Missouri without proper equipment, who failed to travel in large groups for protection against Indians, and keep guards on the job at night, never reached their destination. In 1848 and after, uncounted numbers died of the dreaded cholera, the Asiatic disease which invaded this country at the port of New Orleans and spread up the Mississippi Valley. Ezra Meeker, in his book about his ox-team journey to Oregon, tells of the disease striking his camp. A leader, when asked advice, said, "Now, fellers, don't lose your heads, but do jist as you've been doing. You gals, jist make your bread as light as ever, and we'll take the river water the same as ever, even if it is most as thick as mud, and boil it. . . . Keep cool, maybe we'll have to lay down, and maybe not."

But most of the half-million movers came through alive—even healthier than they started out—and had a fine time to boot. The Oregon volume of the American Guide Series compiled by the Federal Writers' Project states:

. . . for every person who became a symbol of pioneer tragedy there were thousands who thoroughly enjoyed the overland journey. One emigrant who became wealthy remarked wryly in his later years that he suffered more and had less enjoyment on de luxe hunting trips than he had on his oxcart journey across the plains. A Utah woman who had crossed the country about 1850 remembered the trip as a picnic from beginning to end; how she ran beside the slow-moving cart with her arms full of wild flowers; how she and her playmates played hide-and-seek around the wagons; how her mother knitted placidly, day in and day out, and always had time to tell stories; how in the evening the children ran from one campfire to another while their parents gossiped and sang. People quarreled, made love, played cards, danced, wrote poetry and letters, honeymooned, and carried on other normal activities under conditions that gave them added zest.

When the pioneers got to Oregon, two thousand miles from the frontier, they set up their own government. This held until the international boundary was fixed by treaty with Great Britain in 1846 as the forty-ninth parallel. Because of the western settlement, begun by movers over the Oregon Trail, two million square miles of rich land came into the possession of the United States. United politically, the nation became strong; the pioneers on the Oregon

Trail had extended the National Road so that the country, from coast to coast, was held together by the strong band of a trans-continental roadway.

Many of these thousands of movers knew that what they were doing would have its place in American history. They wrote long letters home, and kept diaries. They carved their names in rocks and wrote their names with axle grease on buffalo bones lying on the plains to tell the world: "I went this way!"

15. Road of the Wanderers:
THE MORMON TRAIL

We'll find the place which God for us prepared,
Far away, in the West;
Where none shall come to hurt or make afraid;
There the Saints will be blessed,
We'll make the air with music ring—
Shout praises to our God and King;
Above the rest each tongue will tell—
All is well! all is well!"

Mormon hymn on the journey to Utah

The Mormons, struggling to find a place where they could settle and live without persecution, were the builders of one westward-running road. When they were driven from Independence, Missouri, in 1834, they moved to Illinois and built a new town on a high hill overlooking the Mississippi River. They called the town Nauvoo. There they worked hard and became prosperous, and thought they had found peace at last. But they were wrong; once again they were persecuted and terrorized. Knowing that they would have to move again, the men worked quietly but steadily getting wagons and equipment in readiness. The women prepared wagon covers and tents, dried beef and vegetables, preserved fruit, and sewed warm clothing for the journey.

This time they would go into the western country, and leave forever the territory where they had found no freedom to worship God as they chose. The great exodus was well planned in advance, but the Mormons were forced to leave Nauvoo before they were ready, at a bitter time of year when ice and snow covered the ground.

Driven from behind, they fled across the Mississippi River. On February 4, 1846, the first refugees began crossing the river to Iowa in knocked-together ferries jammed to the edges with cattle, horses, and what food and clothing they had been able to get together hurriedly, their exhausted and untrained pilots dodging the icy river, fighting a cold north wind. On the Iowa side they slowly made their way over the frozen ground nine miles inland through Indian territory to Sugar Creek, which they re-named Brook Kedron, and there formed their first desperate camp. In little more than a week nearly eight hundred families were at the camp, huddled in wagons, tents, and rude shelters of logs and quilts. Many Mormons died that first week.

More refugees arrived at the miserable camp. They had to. "To stay," one of the Mormons said, "is death by fire and sword; to go into banishment unprepared is death by starvation. But yet . . . several hundred of us have started upon our dreary journey. Some of us are already without food, and others have barely sufficient to last a few weeks. . . ."

After February 13 the succeeding groups of emigrants found the going a little easier. The river froze solid, and whole families were able to cross on the ice with what wagons, horses, cattle, and equipment they owned. During that month nearly twelve hundred wagons reached Iowa. The rendezvous at Sugar Creek became crowded, most of the timber was cut for firewood, and many of the wanderers became restless. It was time to leave, to begin the search for a permanent home. On March 1, while hundreds of families were still struggling across from Nauvoo, between two and three thousand people started out from Sugar Creek in five hundred wagons.

They were organized somewhat as an army, according to a plan worked out in Nauvoo more than a year before. Without this plan of movement, they might never have made that journey. One hundred men went ahead to prepare the road and to build crude bridges. There were another hundred riflemen with their commanding officer, another hundred artillery men, also with a commanding officer— and homemade artillery. There were captains of

From Independence, Missouri, in the 1820's, prairie schooners burdened with goods to exchange for Mexico's silver dollars lumbered over desert and plains to beat out the Santa Fe Trail.

The financial panic of 1837 spurred many families in the East to make the two-thousand-mile journey to the lands of promise in the Oregon country. Their migration is an epic of U. S. history.

The Mormons, badgered by persecution, fled from one site to another, finally finding a haven in Utah. The trail they blazed was used later by gold prospectors on the way to California.

The Camel Express, an experiment in hauling goods across the desert, came to an abrupt end when the animals, lonesome for the caravans of their own country, chased terrified mule trains.

The Pony Express, one of the most gallant chapters in the history of the U. S. mails, averaged ten days for the two-thousand-mile run between St. Joseph, Missouri, and Sacramento, California.

On May 10, 1869, an historic occasion took place: The Union Pacific and the Central Pacific railroads joined at Ogden, Utah, thus forming the first railroad link across the continent.

For a time wooden, or plank, roads—made simply by placing planks across the roadbed—rode high in favor. However, they deteriorated quickly, and had to be abandoned since they were not easily repaired.

Such inventions as the steam road-roller, *left,* and Blake's stone crusher, *right,* contributed heavily to the advancement of road-building techniques.

"fifty," and other groups of ten men, each with its leader.

Northwest winds swept hard over those first wayfarers. The cold was intense, the snow, sleet, and driving rain almost unendurable. Many of them, even the strongest, were crippled with frostbite and rheumatism. Their weary work animals could find no nourishment in the prairie straw, bleached by winter, and they turned to eating green bark and branches of cottonwood trees. Hundreds of graves across Iowa marked the road of that first year's journey. The Mormons sorrowfully cut logs in half as coffins for their dead, covered them with bark bound tightly with strong flexible twigs, and mourned because there was no rock to mark the place.

Spring came at last, but with it weeks of heavy rains and melting snow. The prairie road turned to thick black mud, almost impassable. Sometimes, after a day's backbreaking work, the wanderers had covered only a half-mile. Along the road the Mormons established small resting places where blacksmiths were stationed to repair wagons, and where religious leaders awaited the followers. In mid-April the leaders of the migration built a real camp, which they called "Garden Grove." There they dug wells, built log cabins, and planted seeds to grow into a harvest for those farther back on the road.

Men were left to take care of the camp and tend the fields, a kind of permanent garrison. Farther westward the Mormons built another resting place which they called "Mount Pisgah." There they planted several thousand acres of wheat and vegetables, leaving men to care for the camp, as before.

There was never in the United States any migration like this one. Other groups, such as the pioneers on the Oregon Trail, banded together for safety and scattered at the end of the road. They might put up a sign for followers—"Help Yourself" —when they discarded possessions along the road, and they helped each other; but they had no real concern for those who followed them or for those who were ahead. The Mormon migration was different: always on the long journey there were men who went ahead building the road, building bridges and flatboats to haul heavy wagons across unfordable streams. And always there were men who halted to plant seed and harvest crops for the large migration.

By the middle of May their wagons, clustered with horses, cattle, and sheep, stretched all across the territory that is now the state of Iowa. By June the Pioneers (as the Mormons called those leading the trek) had reached the Missouri River. On the east side of the Missouri they set up a camp called Kanesville.

When the Mexican War broke out, the United

States government sent an agent to recruit soldiers from the wandering Mormons, and their leader, Brigham Young, went back along the road, helping the officer obtain enlistments. The young men who composed what was called the Mormon Battalion left the migration and marched to Fort Leavenworth for uniforms and arms. Then, under the charge of the officer who had recruited them, they marched away on foot down the long Santa Fe Trail.

On the west side of the Missouri, the Mormons built another camp. With their young men gone, they decided to stay where they were until spring. This camp, built where Omaha, Nebraska, now stands, they called "Winter Quarters."

Pottawatomie Indians, uprooted from their homes by the white man, lived in these bottom lands of the Missouri. The Indian exiles welcomed the wandering white men who had also been driven from home. Thomas Kane reported the speech of Pied Riche, the Indian chief, to the Mormons:

The Pottawatamie came, sad and tired, into this unhealthy Missouri Bottom not many years back, when he was taken from his beautiful country beyond the Mississippi, which had abundant game and timber and clear water everywhere. You are driven away the same, from your lodges and lands there, and the graves of your people. So we have both suffered. We must help one another, and the Great Spirit will help us both. You are now free to cut and use all the wood you may wish. You can make all your improvements, and live on any part of our actual land not occupied by us. . . .

In return the Mormons helped the Indians with their teams, but in spite of this mutual arrangement the months spent in Winter Quarters from August, 1846, to July, 1847, were a heartbreaking time for the wanderers. They called their camp site "Misery Bottoms," and lived there in crude log huts, tents, shelters made of branches and mud, and even in caves dug from the hillsides. Their chief food was corn meal, and many died that winter from undernourishment and malaria.

Kane wrote about the terrible life at Winter Quarters:

The Mormons were scourged severely. The few who were able to keep their feet went about among the tents and wagons with food and water, like nurses through the wards of an infirmary. Here at one time the digging got behind hand; burials were slow; and you might see women sit in the open tents keeping the flies off their dead children. . . .

Out of six thousand people who had crossed the Missouri to Winter Quarters, six hundred died that winter.

The hard winter passed and spring came again. A Pioneer exploring party struck out for the Rocky Mountains to find a site for their new home. There were 143 men, three women and two children, and seventy-three wagons drawn by oxen and horses in the party, led by Brigham Young.

The Pioneers lived on as rigid a schedule as soldiers. They awoke each morning at five o'clock to the sound of a bugle, ate breakfast, prayed, and were ready to move—wagons, animals, and all—within two hours. Every ten miles or so they put up guide-posts, and wrote messages on them for those who would follow. The little band marched through Nebraska to the Grand Island on the Platte River. Instead of using the Oregon Trail on the south side of the river, they branched off and blazed their own road, now known as the Mormon Trail, to Fort Laramie. Here the Mormon Pioneers rejoined the Oregon Trail until they reached Fort Bridger in Wyoming. They went on, traveling southwest through Echo Canyon, to the Weber River and on toward the ascent of East Canyon. Although they knew that the California land was beautiful, their destination was the less desirable Utah region where they might find peace in country no one else wanted.

When the Mormons caught their first glimpse of the valley of the Great Salt Lake, the lake itself shone like silver in the distance, and high mountains rose on the horizon. It was the Land of Promise to them. The small band had come more than a thousand miles, blazing most of their own roads as they went. They set up camp, unhitched and fed their horses and cattle, dedicated the valley to the Lord, and unpacked their plows from the wagons. One hour later they were turning up the earth to plant seed for autumn crops.

It was October when they finally got back to the Missouri River to tell the good news; it took another few years for the rest of the band to reach the Land of Promise in Utah. Some, in the Handcart Expedition, pushed and pulled their small wheeled vehicles for the thousand miles from Missouri to Salt Lake City.

They were scarcely settled in their "State of Deseret" before gold was discovered in California. In fact, their own young men of the Mormon Battalion, returning home, first brought the news eastward, carrying nuggets as proof. But Mormons would have none of it. They stayed in Utah, which was not designed to incite envy, planted grain, and built a city.

16. LONG ROADS TO GOLD

Did you ever hear tell of sweet Betsy from Pike,
Who crossed the wide prairies with her lover Ike,
With two yoke of cattle and one spotted hog,
A tall shanghai rooster, an old yaller dog?

They swam the wide rivers and crossed the tall peaks,
And camped on the prairie for weeks upon weeks.
Starvation and cholera and hard work and slaughter,
They reached California spite of hell and high water.
"Sweet Betsy from Pike"

When the first Concord stagecoach of the Butterfield Overland Mail rolled into San Francisco in 1858, the town went wild. Its citizens were as excited as New Yorkers had been thirty-eight years earlier when the first boat from the Erie Canal pulled into New York Harbor. The stage driver racing into San Francisco blew his horn as he whipped around the corner of Market Street, cracked his whip, and dashed along Montgomery Street in a cloud of dust behind flying horses, past hundreds of cheering people. No wonder there was such excitement—Californians had waited a long time for regular mail.

The Overland Mail was a tremendous success, the

first "through-route" stagecoach line carrying passengers and the U. S. Mail from the Mississippi River to California. The road it followed led for 2,729 miles from St. Louis, Missouri, through Arkansas to El Paso, Texas, then across New Mexico to Yuma, Arizona, and on into California through Los Angeles and San Francisco. The distance itself was a tremendous problem, but to John Butterfield, owner of the line, distance was a challenge. He had operated a livery stable, an eastern stage company, and a line of Erie Canal packet boats. He had even established a freighting business, hauling gold across the Isthmus of Panama.

Butterfield set up relay stations every ten or fifteen miles on this long road through desert country. Workmen hauled water, hay, and grain for miles to these stations, where men with guns guarded constantly against surprise attack by hostile Indians. For two and a half years (until the Civil War interrupted it) the drivers of this southern stage line maintained a regular schedule over thousands of miles of plains and desert. Each week an Overland Mail coach left California for Missouri, and each week another coach left Missouri for the West. The drivers, keeping a watchful eye for robbers, or Apache and Comanche Indians, got their mail stages through, and delivered their passengers safely—passengers who were willing to pay two hundred dollars, meals extra, and ride twenty-five continuous days, night and day, sitting upright in coaches or hanging grimly to the top.

The discovery of gold in California had sent the first rush of people streaming to the West. Some of the adventurers traveled to California by ship around South America; others quit ship at Panama and made a weary portage on foot across the Isthmus, continuing northward by sea again to the gold fields. But most of the gold-seekers traveled overland. Roads were ready for them: the traders' road to Santa Fe, the movers' road to Oregon, and the Mormons' road to Salt Lake City. Many of the "Forty-niners" used parts of the Oregon Trail and the Mormon Trail to Salt Lake City, then cut through the plains and the Sierra Nevada Mountains into California. This route, first known as the "California Trail," became a wagon road later and was called simply the "Overland Trail." Others in the gold rush were able to reach their Eldorado by following the Santa Fe Trail and then pushing on across the painted deserts of Arizona into the gold fields.

In the first rush twenty thousand men jumped off from Missouri in April, 1849, and many thousands more left the next month. They made the long journey in wagons, on horseback, and afoot, often without any real idea of the heat, dust, and thirst that would torment them on the southern Santa Fe route, or of the crags, snows, and hunger of the northern mountain passes.

Appleton Harmon, traveling overland the following year, made this entry in his diary in 1850:

> We met a continual Stream of Emegration from the mines running meny of them half prepaird frantick mad Crasey or distracted . . . We met a hardy Scotch man with his all upon a wheel barrow going to the gold mines, he had traveled in this way one thousand miles and felt encouraged with the prospects before him and fully believed that he could make the journey in that way. and said he could travel as fast as eney of the horses or mule teams—that he never lost eney Sleep for fear of a stampeed or of his hosses being Stole by the Indians.

Business boomed in San Francisco, but like all boom towns it was shabby and many of its people were rowdy and lawless. Gambling dens lined the streets; robbery and murder were everyday happenings. Soon peaceful citizens became alarmed and formed Vigilance Committees to police the gold country, keep roughnecks in hand, and drive away outlaws.

Californians, in those early days, had another

worry: roads had not yet caught up with them, and mail deliveries from the East took too long. They set up an immediate and loud outcry for better mail service. Letters or newspapers were sent out to California by steamer only twice a month. A high black pole, attached to the top of the tallest building in San Francisco, was the mail signal. Its "arms," by their position, indicated the nature of the cargo of an approaching vessel—in horizontal position meant that a Pacific Mail Company's side-wheel steamer was coming into harbor. At the sign of this black cross in the sky reporters rushed to the steamer to get the latest news from the East for their papers and nearly everybody else made a dash for the post office, some of them waiting in line all night long.

But while Californians *could* get mail and news, the ocean-to-ocean mail service was no help to the scattered homesteader in the Middle West, or to people living in the little towns and villages that were springing up on the main traveled roads. For these people in 1850 a stagecoach line, under contract with the government to carry the mail, started its run for more than a thousand miles from Missouri to Salt Lake City. At first, by pack horse and light wagons, the mail was delivered once a month in good weather. Each hard journey required a two-months' round trip. Later, as relay stations were built along the road and more horses came to the company's stables, travel time was shortened. Before long another stage line, also irregular in schedule, ran from Salt Lake City into California. Finally, Californians could celebrate the regular service of the Butterfield Overland Mail.

In an effort to rush goods and news to the gold fields of California, an odd experiment was tried in 1857 by Jefferson Davis, then Secretary of War in President Buchanan's cabinet: seventy-four camels imported from the Near East were put to work in the American desert country. Their job was to haul freight through Arizona to Bakersfield, California. The camels, wearing fancy blue saddle blankets with the insignia "U.S.A.," were under the care of an Arab named Hadji Ali. Americans mispronounced the name of this short, happy-go-lucky camel driver, but they made the mispronunciation suit him: he was called "Hi Jolly." Known popularly as the camel express, the freight service had a more pretentious name: The Lightning Dromedary Express.

The camel express came to a rather abrupt end. Bill Keiser, a retired prospector who remembered Hi Jolly, told an Associated Press reporter a few years ago that the camels, lonesome for the caravans of their own country, used to make a dash for mule trains. The terrified mules would throw their ears back and bolt like fury. Immediately, angry prospectors reached for their guns and banged away at

the camels. Quite a few were lost that way, the old
man remembered. When the freight service ended
some of the camels, sold at auction, were bought for
zoos and traveling shows and others were simply
turned loose on the country to shift for themselves.

For years the wandering camels had their little
joke on the Americans who abandoned them—they
used to appear as frightening apparitions by moonlight at lonely prospector or cowboy camps, and
probably provided a good argument in the cause of
temperance. In 1920 a few of the beasts were
sighted, appropriately enough, near Camelback
Mountain in Arizona. Mr. Keiser thought there
might still be some of their descendants wandering
around.

During the 1850's a freighting business was established to haul government supplies over the
plains from Fort Leavenworth to mountain Army
posts. This firm—Russell, Majors and Waddell—
grew to enormous size. In one year, 1858, it hauled
sixteen million pounds of government freight over
the western country. Four thousand men were employed to handle the company's thirty-five hundred
wagons, one thousand mules, and forty thousand
oxen. The next year—when the gold rush to Pikes
Peak had begun—one of the partners, William H.
Russell, became part owner of a stage line called the

Leavenworth and Pikes Peake Express. When this line started losing money, it was bought out by the freighting company, which also absorbed the stage line from St. Joseph to Salt Lake City.

Russell, Majors and Waddell called this reorganized line the Central Overland California and Pike's Peake Express. The stage to California, known simply as the "Central," acquired the proud equipment of the southern Overland Mail, which even the knowing John Butterfield could not keep going in wartime.

These three partners possessed daring and imagination, and they had a good head start on other stage lines operating in the Far West. They might have grown even larger and more important, but one big mistake threw them into bankruptcy: they operated the Pony Express, a financial failure.

In those tense days just before the Civil War, telegraph lines were fast pushing toward each other from California eastward, and through Nebraska westward. But between the two lines was a gap of nearly two thousand miles of open plains and mountain country. The Pony Express bridged this distance and brought East and West ten days closer. For sixteen months, between April, 1860, and October, 1861, young men rode hard with the western mail. The joining of telegraph lines across the continent marked the end of that brilliant revival of the post rider.

The horse-line mail service, although short-lived, was as important in its time as any form of transport in the history of the country. Its record time—seven days and seventeen hours—was made when the Pony Express carried President Lincoln's message to Congress into the West in March, 1861. Straining to exhaustion, the riders relayed over two thousand miles the plea for all the West to remain with the United States in the Civil War just beginning.

The usual time required for the eighty Pony Express riders was ten days. They rode over a straight route from St. Joseph, Missouri, to Sacramento, California, each rider making seventy-five or more miles a day. At the 190 relay stations on the long journey only two minutes were allowed for changing horses. Most of the post riders were youngsters of about eighteen. They carried knives and Colt revolvers as protection against bandits and Indians, and rode night and day through snow, ice, rain, or hot sun, over prairies, mountains, and deserts.

But not enough people could afford the five dollars and a half it cost to send letters by Pony Express (or even the dollar later charged). To keep the riders moving day and night, to maintain station keepers all along the way, and to feed and care for the horses cost vast sums. Russell, Majors and Waddell, having put 200,000 dollars into the venture, went bankrupt.

As the frantic gold rush wore itself out, excited prospectors with mining pans and pick-axes were followed by calmer men and women with axes, plows, and spinning wheels. They weren't going all the way to California. They planned to take up some of the good land that the "Forty-niners" passed by. It was they who felled the trees, broke the ground, and built up the West. As this floodtide of Americans rolled overland, Indian and buffalo country became American farmland, and state after state was added to the Union. By 1860 more than four million people lived in that vast region—farmers, miners, shopkeepers, cattlemen and cowboys, soldiers.

The "winning of the West"—that great stretch of land from the Mississippi to the Pacific Ocean, from Canada south to Mexico and the Gulf—took only the thirty years between 1820 and 1850. It is an amazing feat when we consider it had taken more than two hundred years for the white race to establish its civilization across one-third of the American continent as far west as the Mississippi River.

A desire for trade with a foreign land, a terrible depression, a religious crusade, and a fever for gold—all these things pushed Americans into the Far West. They made roads in haste and desperation—the Santa Fe Trail, the Oregon Trail, the Mormon Trail, the Overland Trail—and the homesteaders quietly followed.

17 . ROADS OF THE WESTERN WORLD

"The Star of Empire," poets say, Ho! Westward Ho!
"Forever takes its onward way!" Ho! Westward Ho!
That this be proven in our land, Ho! Westward Ho!
It seems Jehovah's great command, Ho! Westward Ho!

    Ho! Westward! Soon the world shall know
    That all is grand in the western land
        Ho! Westward Ho!

                   (Chorus)
Tis ever thus, the people cry, Ho! Westward Ho!
And from the Eastern cities fly, Ho! Westward Ho!
To live on God's most glorious land, Ho! Westward Ho!
Where hearts and thoughts are ever grand! Ho! Westward Ho!
Ossian E. Dodge

Towns were growing fast all over the West during the 1860's and '70's. Whenever gold or silver was discovered a mining camp sprang up near by. Some of these settlements survived for only a few brief noisy years, to become ghost towns as the mines ran out; other frontier towns grew into thriving cities.

Hundreds of Army forts on river banks, on the plains, and in the mountain passes served as resting places for those making a long wagon journey, and as protection against Indian attack for homesteaders who located nearby.

Thousands of miles of roads connected the young towns and settlements of the western World. They were long roads, running sometimes for hundreds of miles through uninhabited country, for the West because of its vast area was still sparsely settled. Stagecoaches were everywhere, fine, gaily-colored coaches, the last word in luxury travel over the western mountains and prairies. Ben Holliday, called grandly the "Napoleon of the Plains," operated five thousand miles of coach lines. His Overland Stage Line to California, on a daily schedule over the central route, was the most important stage line in the world.

Many trans-continental travelers reached the Mississippi by the National Pike, took a steamboat down the river to St. Joseph, Missouri, and continued to California by the Overland Stage. Inflation caused by the Civil War jumped the customary two-hundred-dollar fare to five hundred dollars.

Four or six matched prancing horses pulled the fine coaches in and out of towns; mules did the hard pulling over the desert. Mark Twain, who made a journey by Overland Stage in 1861, described the desert stretch:

. . . forty memorable miles of bottomless sand, into which the coach wheels sank from six inches to a foot. We worked our passage most of the way across, that is, we got out and walked. It was a dreary pull and a long and thirsty one, for we had no water.

Except for the ever-present danger of attack by highwaymen and Indians, the hardy cross-country travelers could enjoy their journey, for before their speeding coaches spread some of the most majestic scenery in the world. They crossed the grassy rolling plains of Kansas already brightened by hundreds of tall corn fields, and went on toward the Platte River, following closely a road worn deep by the wagon wheels of the movers to Oregon some twenty-five years earlier. Their road branched again, following the Mormon Trail, and continued westward over what had been called the "California Trail" in the days of the gold rush.

Horses were changed every ten or fifteen miles, and "home stations" of log or stone were spaced at intervals of fifty miles. Here drivers finished their runs, and passengers ate and rested. These frontier stations were far different from the taverns of the East. The stationmaster wore a woolen shirt and country-style britches reinforced with buckskin. Always alert to danger from Indians and outlaws, he kept within trigger-finger reach a revolver; and a bowie-knife dangled from his belt.

The always-watchful Indians became violent during the years when the United States was busy with its Civil War. Once they attacked and killed the two keepers at the station in Nevada just beyond the Utah line. Then they hid and waited to plunder the Overland Stage driving in from the west. Hank Harper, the driver, knew when he was seventy feet or so away that something was wrong because the station was so quiet. He tried to turn his coach aside, but was hit by an Indian bullet. A second bullet hit one of his passengers. Another passenger, a Nevada delegate to Congress, grabbed the lines. The dying stage driver gave directions and encouragement as long as he could, and the stage managed to get safely to the next station.

When the Civil War ended, use of the southern stage line was resumed, and once more people living in the Southwest could travel on the "Butterfield" route between the Mississippi River and California. Many other stage lines began operation within and between states, and soon a network of roads laced together hundreds of settlements. These roads were also much used by Conestogas; for wagon hauling, long dead in the East, came to life and riches in the West—a prosperity which lasted until trains replaced them. Pack horses were used for many years in difficult country where wagons could not pass.

Another kind of road business which developed early was the express. Most of the overland stages had special "express" coaches, always a jump ahead of government mail service in delivering packages and letters to the last frontiers. The express stages carried in their "strongboxes" most of the gold dust, money, and valuable packages moving between the East and the West. The strongbox was placed beneath the driver's seat, and it was traditional for him to defend it with his life. The Wells-Fargo Company, organized in 1852, bought out other California express companies, and became the biggest stage line and express company along the West Coast. In time Wells-Fargo stages were speeding all over the West.

Highwaymen and bandits, called "road agents," made the stage driver's job a peril. These outlaws operated over almost every stage road in the West. If necessary they murdered to obtain the strongbox and rob passengers. The stories of near-escapes and holdups became legend, and are still being used as themes for western movies. Charles Michelson, in *Stage Robbers of the West*, tells of Sidney Jake, a road agent who once shot a driver, marched the passengers away from the coach, robbed them of money and weapons, then went back to the coach, took the gloves from the body of the dead driver, and drove the empty stage into town. There he picked up a load of passengers and the strongbox, drove out of town, and proceeded to rob the mail, the box, and the second load of passengers, after which he killed all the horses except the one he used to ride away, carrying well-filled saddlebags.

Then there is the story of Charley Parkhurst, a small but quick-thinking stage driver, never outwitted by robbers. One highwayman caught the whip on his face just as he jumped from the brush, and was blinded in one eye. Another highwayman tried to grab a horse's bridle and stop the coach, but Parkhurst lashed the horse so that it reared and knocked the robber over a bridge. He shot at Parkhurst as the coach rattled down the mountain, but missed. It was not until he died many years later that it was discovered Parkhurst was a woman, a widow with a daughter in an eastern finishing school.

During the sixties two railroads started building toward each other to form the first railway link across the continent, the Union Pacific westward from Omaha, and the Central Pacific toward the east from San Francisco. It was hard work, and made constantly more difficult by harassment from the Indians. Food was plentiful, however, in the buffalo country, and the bones of the animals who had provided meat for the railroad builders piled up along the new track for hundreds of miles. The gigantic task of building the railroad took seven years and twenty-five thousand workmen. Finally, on May 10, 1869, the tracks came together at Ogden, Utah. Except for the Wells-Fargo Company, it was a day of celebration all along the line.

Because of the railroads, a new kind of dirt road developed in the West—the cattle trails. Three and a half million head of cattle overstocked Texas when the Civil War cut off northern markets, and the ranch owners became "cattle poor." After the war, when trains began pushing westward, the ranchers realized what it meant to them—their cattle could travel east by rail.

Hundreds of miles of trail, from two to four hundred yards wide, led to the railway shipping centers. One of these centers was Abilene, Kansas—a wise choice, for the rich prairie grass was good for herds waiting to be shipped. Other railroad terminals were at Newton, Wichita, and Dodge City.

The "Chisholm Trail" was named for the man who first drove his cattle over it to the railroad at Abilene, six hundred miles away. The "Old Shawnee Trail" led to Baxter Springs, Kansas. There were other trails, too, and before long middle Kansas looked like an enormous cattleyard. In one year, 1871, the Texas cowboys drove nearly a million cattle into Kansas. The trails became sunken and hard-packed from the constant tramping of animals.

Many a song was sung by the cowboys on those roads, but not the guitar-accompanied tunes we think of today as typical cowboy fare. Trail songs were called hymns in those days (frequently they really were hymns), and they were sung for a purpose. The cowboy guard at night had to sing to his cattle when they started to mill, to reassure the beasts with the familiar, quieting sound of the human voice. Besides the usual singing profanity, the cowboys made up ballads, or told the unruly animals in song exactly what they thought of them. When the cowboys ran out of lyrics and imagination they sang, to the tune of hymns, the words taken from labels on cans of condensed milk.

Within fifteen years of the joining of the rails between the East and the West, six companies were operating railroads on a network of tracks all over the West. The railroads brought people into the region in astonishing numbers—the times of the slow-moving oxcarts and covered wagons were over. Within thirty years, nearly two million people made the western journey to find new homes on the other side of the Rocky Mountains. Trains had taken over the big job of hauling freight and passengers, and soon wagons were used only on local trips or to railroad depots.

Where there were railroad tracks no roads were built, but stagecoaches, of course, continued to carry passengers and mail wherever railroads didn't penetrate; and pack horses continued to haul supplies where stage and wagon roads ended.

AMERICA ON
WHEELS

18. BUGGIES AND BICYCLES

. . . We won't have a stylish marriage,
I can't afford a carriage,
But you'll look sweet
Upon the seat
Of a bicycle built for two.

"Daisy Bell"

The buggy gave its name to the last half of the nineteenth century because of its raging popularity. With its hickory shafts, leather through-braces, and up-or-down hood, it was far more comfortable and practical than the two-wheeled chaise, from which it developed, and it became as much a part of American life as the family car is today.

Roads in the United States were in miserable condition at the time. The National Pike, long since back in the hands of the states through which it ran, had fallen into almost complete disrepair. After the Civil War, the United States government had stopped building roads; it maintained the streets of Washington, D. C., and the few miles of thorough-fares leading to national cemeteries from near-by towns—and that was all. With the government out of the road-building business, control went to the local governments. The confusion that resulted is hard to imagine. One county would build a road right up to its line, but the next county might see fit to build its roads in a different direction—with the result that frequently no "through road" joined them.

Actually, the history of roads had repeated itself: the country was back to the system of statute labor which had been followed in colonial days. This meant that there was a road tax, and a citizen paid the tax by getting out on the road digging and scraping dirt, or paying someone else to do the job for him. "Working out the road tax" got to be a joke, it was so shabbily done.

Most of the roads had been built over Indian trails, pig paths, or the wandering line from one settler's cabin to another. In the West they often ran along "section" lines, and since the sections were square, the roads would be straight for a distance, then zig-zag right and left. Over the years a great deal of time and hard work were spent on the almost hopeless job of trying to improve these old lines of travel.

Another reason for the deplorable state of American roads was that trains had captured the imagination of the people—*rail* roads were more important than *common* roads, as the routes for horse-drawn vehicles were called. People who had money to invest put it into railway lines. Most of the private turnpike companies went bankrupt, for there was not enough toll-paying traffic to support the roads.

With so many people depending indirectly on roads for a living, it is surprising that there were no good ones. The manufacture of family vehicles was in itself a large industry. Livery stables were everywhere, and horseshoes and nails were turned out by the thousands. Express carriages and hacks for hire met most of the trains. Harness-makers did a tremendous business. So did saddlers, especially in wartime when they were swamped with government orders for cavalry.

There were many related industries. Some factories specialized in fine cloth and plushes for carriages, others made sleighbells, still others horsewhips. By 1855 Westfield, Massachusetts, had thirty factories manufacturing horsewhips. Eight leading factories in that year turned out whips costing altogether nearly 300,000 dollars.

Some effort to improve the roads was made in the early years, however, and one of the first steps was the building of wooden roads. For a time there was almost a mania for wooden, or plank roads—made by simply placing planks lengthwise across the roadway. This procedure was fairly easy, especially in those parts of the country thick with trees and sawmills.

Plank roads were used first in Russia, and on this continent in Canada. Then, in 1846, New York State began the plank-road craze in the United States by building such a road from Syracuse to Oneida Lake. Everywhere private companies, caught in the plank-road craze, turned to building wooden toll roads. In Wisconsin alone there were 135 such companies. But the wooden roads decayed after a few years, and were dangerous to travel. Many companies abandoned their plank roads rather than repair them, and the dark ages of the roads grew darker.

Most roads were so bad that it cost farmers as much to get their goods to a railway station (usually about ten miles away) as to pay for four hundred miles of shipment by rail. Worse than that, farmers could take their goods to the stations only in good weather when roads were passable, and for this reason the railroads themselves were getting in bad shape. Hundreds of thousands of freight cars were empty for weeks at a time, and then, when the weather improved, were jammed with more freight than they could carry.

It remained for the riders of another kind of vehicle to start a Good Roads Movement. They were the bicyclists.

As soon as sturdy, safe bicycles were put on the market, a fad for bicycle riding hit the country, and cycling clubs mushroomed everywhere. For the

Cycling became a craze around the turn of the century. Clubs all over the country sprang up, and their members set up a loud outcry for better roads over which to ride their vehicles.

The early motor car was not known for its durability, and often the motorist spent more time under his automobile than behind its wheel, to the amusement and jibes of spectators.

Rural road in Missouri in 1905, showing the ruinous effects of rains on dirt surfaces. Conditions such as this prompted the cry for roads that would "Get the farmer out of the mud!"

By 1916, gravel and other hard-surfaced roads provided rural motorists with reasonable assurance of all-weather travel.

Thirty-five years ago the principal highway between Richmond, Virginia, and Washington, D. C., looked like this. The building is Pohick Church, where George Washington worshiped.

Today, travel between the two cities is speeded by this four-lane highway, an important stretch of U. S. 1. Note same church in background.

In the early days of motoring, before an integrated system of road building was worked out by the states, a motorist often found that the paved highway he was traveling ended abruptly at the state line.

Notable steps forward in highway improvement were the adoption of uniform signs, and various experiments, such as the pneumatic tire impact test.

first time in history people were able to travel safely on wheels using their own power, independent of horses and steam engines.

Bicycles had been regarded with suspicion at first, and frequently were forbidden on streets and parkways. Enthusiastic wheelmen, however, were not to be stopped. They were particularly proud of the "Liberty Bill," passed in 1887, which gave New York cyclists the right to ride through Central Park, and on every city street.

On Sundays and holidays, all over the United States, parks and streets were crowded with gay excursionists. During the "Gay Nineties," more than four million Americans owned wheels and rode them at every chance. The men wore small caps, Norfolk jackets, baggy knee-length knickers, and woolen socks. Women cyclists had a costume, too: short skirts or bloomers, shirtwaists, and straw sailors.

The bicycle had a practical value also, as working women in Philadelphia found out during a streetcar strike which was called during the winter of 1895–96. Downtown streets were crowded with bicycles. "The weather was very cold," *Munsey's Magazine* reported, "and many of the riders carried their hands in muffs, guiding the wheels by slight movements of the body. Clerks in stores, typewriters, and the whole great army of employed women rode their wheels to business; women who came to buy left bicycles in the checkrooms of the great shops."

The safety bicycle, similar to modern ones, developed curiously from the hobby horse of 1819. The hobby horse—which in France was called a celeripede—had a seat, handlebars, and two wheels, but no pedals. The rider simply sat in the saddle and pushed along with his feet, as does a baby in a "kiddy car" today. In another thirty years or so the "boneshaker" came along. This heavy wooden bicycle with its iron tires—and complete lack of springs—earned its name. Later the dangerous high-wheeled "ordinary" took the place of the boneshaker; and from this spindly bicycle grew the safety. By 1885 the safety was the bicycle of the day.

Bicycle racing as an organized sport was the sensation of the times, and was given as much coverage by newspapers as football and baseball today. The members of the American World Racing Team of 1897, having won honors throughout Europe, were given the homage due heroes when they returned to the sports-loving United States. Speeding, called "scorching" in the Gay Nineties, was forbidden in town, and bicycle speeders went out into the country. So did a number of more leisurely wheelmen and women who wanted fresh air and a change of scenery. But the roads were so terrible that it was almost impossible to cycle far, even in good weather. Another worry to the cyclists out in the country was the lack of road signs. Signposts hadn't been needed until then, for farmers and their families living near by knew their directions, and few other persons used the roads.

Cycle clubs all over the country set up a loud outcry for better roads. They organized a national group called The League of American Wheelmen, published their own magazines, and started the Good Roads Movement. Finally the Federal government set up an Office of Roads Inquiry under the Department of Agriculture. The Office found, for one thing, that railroads were eager to haul material to build better "common" roads, in order to improve their own position.

In 1903 President Theodore Roosevelt spoke out:

We should have a right to ask that this people which has tamed a continent, which has built up a country with a continent for its base, which boasts itself with truth as the mightiest Republic the world has ever seen . . . we should have a right to demand that such a nation build good roads.

Badly hit by the lack of good common roads, the railroads began sending out "Good Roads" trains into the countryside. These caravans organized "Good Roads" clubs, held "Good Roads" conventions, and frequently built a sample road to show what could be done. The Southern Railway, really in earnest, furnished a "Good Roads" caravan composed of ten to twelve cars jammed with road-making machinery, another car for laborers, and two private cars for "Good Roads" headquarters. The railway held conventions in eighteen places, and built sample roads ten or twelve miles long. On the convention floor with the railroads, making speeches for better roads, were state governors, congressmen, senators, and presidents of universities, as well as the businessmen and farmers who would be directly benefited.

States tried to do something to help, too. New Jersey had started the ball rolling in 1891 with its State Aid Road Law, and one state after another followed the example. They got their counties to work together so that all the roads in the state would "match," and not end with county lines.

These small beginnings, encouraged by cyclists, at least interested people in roads. But it took something a lot bigger than a bicycle to get fine highways all over the country. This was a job waiting for the automobile. Already the first ones were being made.

19. NO PUSHING AND
NO PULLING

"Fanatical opposition to the automobile is on the whole very rare in this country. The metropolitan dailies occasionally print strong editorials denouncing speed excesses and careless driving, but the whole press is practically unanimous in recognizing the automobile as a legitimate pleasure vehicle and as destined to a great future in the commercial world. . . . "It is, of course, unfortunate that horse drivers in districts little frequented by automobiles should be so much annoyed by the advent of the new vehicle, but all progress is accompanied by obstacles and annoyances, and cursing progress will not stem its tide.

Editorial in The Horseless Age *(1903)*

As might be expected, early automobiles looked like buggies. Usually the seats were high above the wheels, the one- or two-cylinder engines in the back. There was no top, and not even a windshield at first, and the engines made so much noise and the machinery clattered so loudly that passengers had to shout at each other to be understood.

The automobile had been an idea for more than a hundred years, and men had successfully rigged up carriages and various odd contraptions with steam-engines. Even when the first automobile appeared in the 1890's it was an unsettled question which force would move it: steam, electricity, or gasoline. As early as 1830 a steam carriage had been developed in England which ran at a speed of ten miles an hour and carried fourteen people. But the resistance of stagecoach companies and of the public whose horses were frightened by the noise and smoke put an end to the growth of the horseless carriage in England. France and Germany continued experimenting, and by 1892 had developed the automobile (the word itself is of French origin).

In the United States the automobile pioneers were Charles Duryea, Elwood Haynes, Ranson E. Olds, and Henry Ford. The first gasoline automobile was driven down the streets of Springfield, Massachusetts, in 1892 by Charles and Frank Duryea. Soon Henry Ford had his first car on the streets of Detroit, and it was a great curiosity. "If I stopped the machine anywhere in town," Ford said, "a crowd was around it before I could start it again. If I left it for a moment, someone always tried to run it. Finally I had to carry a chain and tie it to a lamp-post whenever I left it anywhere."

For years automobiles were used only for pleasure driving in spring and summer when roads and streets were passable. With the coming of winter they were stored away, as were other seasonal possessions such as boats, lawn mowers, straw hats, and tennis racquets. Garages then were called automobile stables. In good weather when a family was able to "take out" the car, roads and streets were so dusty that special motoring clothes were essential. Men wore goggles and women covered their faces and big hats with heavy veils. Both wore long flowing linen coats called "dusters."

Learning to drive early cars was catch-as-catch can. Dr. O. F. Hess of western Pennsylvania, proud owner of a "steam machine," offered this advice to readers of *The Horseless Age* in 1903:

> Let me say here to those who are about to sell their horses and buy an automobile that they should keep enough horse sense to run it. It requires just a little horse sense to operate and take care of a horseless wagon . . . If you have no one to teach you how to operate your machine—and you really don't need anyone—take the machine into the back yard and study the use of every bolt, nut, pin, wheel, valve, and lever, look into every hole and corner in the machine and master the mechanism of all its vital parts, then fill up the tanks and light the fire.

The doctor advised trying out the machine at midnight by the light of a full moon, when all "vulgar vehicles" were off the road. "If you have a bosom friend," he added pointedly, "a strong man of a taciturn mind, you might take him along. You may need him."

Not enough people had the courage to light the fire of the steam machine, and before long gasoline buggies led the field. Ranson Olds, by 1903, was selling four thousand cars a year. They weighed seven hundred pounds and cost 650 dollars, and were so popular there was a song about his car, "My Merry Oldsmobile."

With this head start in mass production, the Oldsmobile might have led the field; but the company decided there was more money to be made in higher-priced cars. Henry Ford, however, liked the idea of producing thousands of cheap cars. He put his famous Model T on the market in 1908. It was a lightweight, cheap car easy to repair and easy to drive, and soon there were more Model T's on the road than any other car. They were affectionately called "Tin Lizzies."

The automobile driver of today would be appalled if he had to take his car over the roads faced by early motorists—the first automobiles rattled over surfaces that were not even good enough for buggies and wagon teams. Most of them were made of earth, the worst possible material; but earth where it is costs nothing. In 1904, when the government took the first road census, there were two million miles of plain dirt roads. In summer months they were dusty and bumpy, although passable. At other times they were "bottomless" with mud. Newfangled road rollers and scrapers were of little real help.

Progressive cities and communities surfaced their main streets and important through-roads with gravel and stone, and these were the best in the country. Out of two million miles of roads, only 141 miles were "hard"-surfaced with tar, asphalt, or brick, and only 153,664 miles of roads in the whole United States were "improved."

Some of the "improvements" seem odd today, but at that time the few road builders tried any material they thought would give a road a solid bottom. Roads were even made of sawdust. Men working out the road tax spread eight or ten inches of sawdust over the roadbed, then covered it with sand. The sand was important, for it kept the road from catching on fire if someone carelessly threw away a lighted pipe or stogy. Sawdust roads lasted four or five years, and were thought to be very fine indeed. They were much in use in the 1890's, and even for many years after.

More durable roads made of a mixture of sand and clay were built, particularly in the South. They furnished a fairly solid surface for wagon teams hauling heavy bales of cotton. In the lower Mississippi Valley, where the soil is all clay, the roadway was made of clay and then set on fire to remove the "stickiness." These, naturally, were called burnt-clay roads. This method of obtaining a hard surface did not develop in the United States. As early as 800 B. C. burnt-clay roads were made in India, and only recently Australia revived the ancient system.

Other roads were made entirely of sand, which had to be kept damp and moist—quite the opposite of dirt roads, where the problem was to keep them dry. Motorists also had to contend with old-time corduroy roads, especially in swampy and timbered areas. Even oyster shells were used in road construction, particularly along the eastern seaboard and in southern states where there were no stones to be had. Maryland had 250 miles of "shell" roads. "So far as beauty is concerned," the government Office of Roads Inquiry reported to farmers, "they cannot be surpassed."

Almost from the beginning the states passed speed laws, usually from eight to ten miles an hour in town to fifteen miles an hour in the country. Horse-drawn vehicles had right of way, and automobiles had to slow down or come to a complete stop when meeting the former. On narrow roads, the automobile was expected to go off the surface and wait for the wagon or buggy to pass. The Maine law for 1903 read in part ". . . racing is prohibited. . . . Bells or other appliances for giving notice of approach, which may be heard at a distance of 300 feet, shall be carried on all automobiles, and also a lighted lamp between one hour after sunset and one hour before sunrise."

Automobile drivers were concerned chiefly with getting out of the mud, and they became fairly expert in overcoming the hazards of bad roads. They had to know how to combat not only the mud, but ruts, ditches, and dust. Instinctively, too, as if the trick had been passed down by stagecoaching ancestors of a hundred years before, motor passengers leaned to right or left to preserve balance.

Many drivers carried wooden planks, placed them under the car wheels when stuck in the mud, drove or pushed the car the distance of the plank, got out, moved the plank forward—and by repeating this long enough were usually able to get rolling again. Often they took along lengths of strong rope, which came in handy. Motorists frequently had to stop a farmer working in his field, or hail a passing wagon driver, hire a team of horses, and come out of the mud pulled by the horses and their own stout rope.

In 1908 there were only 650 miles of macadam roads in the entire country, and no concrete roads at all. There were no road maps and directions given were hit-or-miss. *The Horseless Age* in that year reported these directions for getting from Albuquerque to Los Angeles: "Follow this mountain range eighty miles south to a stick in the fork of a road, with a paper tied to the top. Take the rut that leads off to the right."

The automobile was getting sturdier all the time, automobile owners were becoming more confident of their ability, less fearful that they would break down. Automobile clubs and manufacturers encouraged this attitude by holding "reliability runs," starting as early as 1900. Sometimes these automobile tests were spectacular, and almost always they were big social events. One of the first, scheduled to run from New York to Buffalo along the Hudson and Mohawk rivers, was called off because of the assassination of President McKinley. In 1903 the National Association of Automobile Manufacturers proved that their cars could go some distance from automobile stables: those wobbly models—the ones that came through to win—made the "endurance" run from New York to Pittsburgh, through Buffalo and Cleveland, in eight days, covering 793 miles.

A motoring enthusiast named Charles J. Glidden offered a fine trophy for the winner of an annual endurance and racing event, to be sponsored by the American Automobile Association. The Glidden Tours demonstrated that cars could go wherever there were good roads—the 1911 Tour covered the distance of more than a thousand miles between New York and Jacksonville, Florida. But the Tour the following year was postponed because roads were impassable—spring floods had made them rivers of mud.

In the early years help from farmers could not always be counted on by stranded motorists. Some farmers waged active war against the automobile invasion: they stretched chains across the road, set up "speed traps," and held up the motorist at the point of a gun. Others charged outrageous prices for the goods and services that motorists were forced into buying from them.

Around 1910, though, this began to change, for many farmers owned their own cars, particularly in the western prairie country where the long "natural" roads could be used fairly easily in dry weather. Automobiles provided the means of getting farm products to market, and enabled farm children to go farther away from home to better schools. The one-room schoolhouse began to disappear. There were other advantages, too. When roads weren't impassable with mud, doctors could get out into the country quickly and easily, and so could home demonstration agents, who taught farm women modern methods of canning and cooking food, and home decoration.

All over the country farm families bought automobiles as soon as they could scrape together the money for down payment. For the first time women were able to get away from the monotony of their farms, and go to town to shop and visit. When one farm woman was asked why the family owned a car when they had no bathtub in the house, she was surprised at the question and replied, "Why, you can't go to town in a bathtub!"

In Nebraska, Kansas, Missouri, and Iowa automobile engines were put to uses not contemplated by their manufacturers: they turned cream-separators, shelled corn, and supplied the power for family washing! In Wyoming and Idaho the automobile was used to round up herds of cattle.

Motorists had to be their own repairmen, for there were no handy garages. They stowed away in their cars repair parts and spare tires, as well as emergency supplies of gasoline and oil. All were needed—automobiles broke down with such frequency that often the drivers spent more time under the car than riding in it. There were many jokes about this—one tells of a visitor who called upon a friend in an insane asylum, and glanced through the ward designed for motorists whose automobiles had driven them crazy. No one was in sight. "Look under the beds," the attendent explained. "They're all down there repairing the bed slats!"

Paul G. Hoffman, president of the Studebaker

Corporation, tells about a "long" motor trip of sixty miles, taken in the spring of 1909:

. . . I was the chauffeur on the first long motor trip of the Hoffman family. The car was a 1905 Pope-Toledo purchased secondhand by my father at a cost of approximately $1,500. It was an open car. The chassis would have done credit to Rube Goldberg. Advertisements called it the world's first mile-a-minute automobile. Tires cost from $75 to $90 apiece, were good for about 2,500 miles; punctures were frequent. A steering knuckle cost $30, and a new one was needed every so often. Springs, priced at about $30, broke every time you hit a bad bump. There were seven lugs on each wheel; to change a tire was a major operation. For touring we carried sixteen spark plugs, all available inner tubes, two extra casings, tools enough to outfit a small garage.

We lived in Western Springs, southwest of Chicago. Our trip, for which we had to wait until spring, had as its destination Sycamore, Illinois, approximately sixty miles away. Preparations were made weeks ahead. We started bright and early on Saturday morning, with five people and an enormous hamper of lunch. Our adventures, briefed, were as follows:

In the first few miles I changed four spark plugs. Otherwise, everything was lovely.

On the far side of the Fox River I tried to shift from third to second gear to climb a hill, and failed. When the car was out of gear there was no service brake. We started to roll backward. My aunt screamed, tossed out the lunch basket, and followed it herself in a flying leap. I stopped the car by backing into the bank.

After trying again and making the grade, we reached a fork in the road. Nobody knew which one to take, and we had no maps. Father said "left" and Grandfather said "right." Grandpa had the more positive manner, and we went right. We should have gone left.

It began to rain. Considerable time was lost putting up the curtains. The road became a bog in which we finally sank. I cut brush to give the wheels traction. We got out of the first mudhole, went a short way, sank again.

Night came on. I lighted the head lamps. Old-fashioned rock-carbide lamps, they flickered and flickered, went out. No help at all for seeing ahead. We slid into the ditch and were stuck for good. A neighboring farmer gave Mother and Aunt a bed for the night . . .

Next morning we managed to get out of the ditch under our own power. We had come forty-five miles and had had enough; we headed for home.

Presently the engine stopped cold. Trying to crank it, Grandpa gashed his forehead on the sharp toe of the radiator. The cut bled freely. My aunt and my mother began to weep.

I discovered what was wrong with the engine. A valve at the bottom of the crankcase had been turned when we were stuck in the ditch. The oil drained out, the engine "froze." I had extra oil and managed to start the engine, but we had burned out all the bearings, and I found that the engine would die if the car speed dropped below thirty miles per hour.

At St. Charles, where we had started to roll downhill the day before, the two ladies got on the streetcar and went home. The nearest garage was at Aurora, fourteen miles away. We three men headed for it. We struck at least fifty "thank-you-ma'ams" in the road between Aurora and St. Charles, taking them at thirty. Grandpa used most of his vivid vocabulary.

The car stayed in the Aurora garage about a month and was practically rebuilt . . .

Motoring was like that . . .

20. ROAD-BUILDING BOOM

If there is any kind of advancement going on, if new ideas are abroad and new hopes rising, then you will see it by the roads that are building. Nothing makes an inroad without making a road.

Horace Bushnell

Once the road-building and road-improvement began, there was no stopping it. In the twenty years between 1921 and 1941 the face of the United States had changed. A great highway network had developed, the finest in any country in the world. In those years forty billion dollars had been spent on roads, and by 1941 thirty-four million motor vehicles operated over a million and a half miles of surfaced highways. Altogether, three million miles of roads reached into every settled corner in the United States, about a mile of road for every square mile of land in the country.

Deserts and mountains had challenged the road builders, and had been conquered. Mighty bridges, triumphs of modern engineering, crossed the rivers of America, keeping highways continuous. Road signs made direction-finding a simple matter, and road maps could be found at any filling station. Huge, brightly painted buses flashed over the highways carrying America's vacationing tourists and business travelers. Giant trucks hauled tons of goods day and night, north, south, east, and west. The look of thousands of cities, towns, and villages had changed in those twenty years. They had "exploded," some experts said; they had just plain "sprawled out," said others.

The years from the time of the first automobile's appearance until the end of World War I were years of preparation, the small beginnings that paved the way for the big road-building boom of the twenties and thirties. Few people in those early days had the vision to see how vast our highway system would become. They were proud of each firm step, and each in its own way was important.

Wayne County, Michigan, had a right to be proud back in 1909. It had built a fine new road, only one mile long, but made of something new and durable —concrete. The road was the wonder of highway engineers, and they came from all over the United States and Canada to see it. The next year the concrete was spread for another mile, and the good news traveled farther. To see just a couple of miles of concrete in Michigan, delegations of road officials journeyed from all over the world—England, France, Holland, Java, Borneo, Ceylon, South Africa, Japan, Peru, Australia, and New Zealand.

By 1913 more than fifty large "Good Roads" associations, and at least five hundred smaller ones, shouted the cause. Trail associations mushroomed, each wanting its own old trail to be rebuilt or "rediscovered," as they called it. People began to remember the charm—and the real usefulness—of the long-abandoned National Pike. Twenty-four miles of the old road, extending westward from Zanesville, Ohio, were actually drained, graded, and given a Portland cement surfacing. For the first time, on this section of the road at least, automobiles and trucks could travel easily over the ancient route of Indians, buffalo, and pioneers.

About this time Carl G. Fisher of Indianapolis had a daring idea: why not build a good road to cross the continent, from coast to coast? He thought about it, talked about it, and in the fall of 1912 presented the idea to the young automobile industry. Fisher obtained pledges for four million dollars, and named the road for a great president—The Lincoln Highway. The route for the road was chosen: from Jersey City through Philadelphia, Gettysburg, Pittsburgh, Fort Wayne, near Chicago and on through Omaha, Cheyenne, Salt Lake City, and Sacramento to San Francisco, a distance of 3,389 miles. The Lincoln Highway Association was formed, and states and private citizens enthusiastically contributed money —pennies, nickels, dimes, quarters, and hundreds of dollars. Cement manufacturers gave the material for "demonstration miles." Actual work was begun on the road in October, 1914, but it moved westward slowly, as the National Pike had a hundred years earlier.

Water-bound macadam roads were good enough for wagon traffic; but with the coming of World War I, hundreds of trucks hauling equipment for war took to the roads. The pounding of their solid rubber tires was more than the roads could take. In those early days the federal government conducted experiments in road building, helping the states modernize their old lines of travel. This research grew into the comprehensive laboratory and field studies of today's Bureau of Public Roads.

In July, 1916, the federal government returned in earnest to the job of helping the country finance good roads—a job almost entirely neglected since the abandonment of the National Pike. In that year Congress passed the Federal-Aid Road Act, which provided for joint construction by the federal government and the states to improve rural roads used to carry the mail. This was the first big step forward toward good roads, since all important country roads were post roads. There was no more "mud at the state line," since under the provisions of the Act state roads were made to connect with those of adjoining states, just as county roads had been "matched" in the nineties. For the first time the United States had a planned network of roads from Canada south to the Gulf of Mexico, from the Atlantic Ocean to the Pacific.

By the end of World War I there were more than 300,000 miles of surfaced roads. This was good news to the six million families who owned automobiles. They began to think it would be very fine indeed to be able to drive in winter as well as in summer—so manufacturers began to make closed cars. The clamor for good roads continued. A highway engineer in the South wryly hung this sign on his office door in 1924: "I am prepared to admit that the road leading to your doorway is the most important road in the world. Now what else can we talk about?"

None of the roads are the property of the United States government, of course; all belong to the states in which they are located. The U. S. Highways, however, are supported in part by federal money. When you pass the familiar United States Highway shield, black on a white background, designating the number of the highway, you know that you are traveling over an important artery in America's transportation network.

Back in 1921 this system was worked out under the Federal Highway Act: the state highway departments were to pick out the most important interstate and inter-county roads (no more than seven per cent of the existing rural roads) and spend all federal appropriations on building and maintaining these particular routes. Under the Act, the states had full responsibility for maintaining the roads; but if any state let them fall into disrepair, the federal government itself would supervise their maintenance, and pay for it out of government allotments. The roads selected by the states, and partially supported by the federal government, are now known as United States Highways.

The effect of good roads was immediate. North Carolina, for example, spent 125 million dollars on highway construction between 1919 and 1926. Thirteen thousand new farms were started, and forty co-operative farm markets developed, distributing eggs and poultry, fruit, vegetables, and livestock on the hoof, and farm families increased their income by selling produce at roadside markets. All over the state freshly painted barns and farm houses reflected the rising standard of living.

All the states, at the beginning of the twenties, had state highway departments. State and county road systems were designated, and more and more money became available for their building and maintenance from taxes on gasoline and motor vehicle licenses. In the year 1918 three hundred million dollars was spent for highway construction; by 1930, at the beginning of the depression, the annual expenditure had swung upward to one and one-half billions.

In order to provide jobs during the depression, relief agencies of the federal government spent several billion dollars for highway construction, and permitted the money to be used on secondary, or farm-to-market roads, and on through-routes passing over city streets.

By the early thirties it was a simple matter to drive thousands of miles. Most people who planned long trips traveled during good weather, but there were exceptions. The *Saturday Evening Post,* describing the pleasures of driving coast-to-coast, pointed out that it could be done easily, even in *winter,* by taking Route 80, the rediscovered Old Spanish Trail. For two people, this trip in the depression year 1934 cost one hundred dollars, allowing enough for gourmet sampling of native food in good restaurants in each city.

Twenty years earlier, traveling coast-to-coast over good roads had seemed an improbable dream. Now, in the thirties, it could be done. Americans, always itching to go somewhere, always a couple of jumps ahead of their freight lines, began to think that some day it might be possible to drive to Alaska, to Panama, or even to South America.

21. THE YOUNG GIANT

This is the song that the truck drivers hear
In the grinding of brake and the shifting of gear,
From the noise of the wheel and the clarion horn,
From the freight and the weight—a song has been born:
Mohair and cotton and textile and silk,
Chicken and onions and apples and milk,
Rubber and clothing and coffee and tires,
Harness and hay and molasses and wires,
Petroleum, vinegar, furniture, eggs,
Race horses, stoves and containers and kegs,
Chemicals, canteloupes, canned goods and seeds—
Song of the cargo America needs!
Song of the wheels in the well-traveled grooves—
Coastline to coastline—America moves!

"Song of the Truck"

On any night in the year, anywhere be-tween Maine and Florida, Arizona and Washington State, you can see the heavy-shouldered man in the little roadside places that are drowsily awake in the glow of neon signs when almost everything else is closed.

The man is a type and a symbol of something large and growing—but there is nothing dramatic in the sight of him. He simply hunches forward on the counter stool and asks for a second hunk of pie or a third cup of coffee. He swallows it, says something like, "Well, I've got to be hittin' the road again," and is gone. The full roar of a motor comes for a moment from the dark roadside beyond the door and then fades into a murmur in the distance. There are about five million American truck drivers, descendants in spirit of the men who drove the rumbling Conestogas.

When we think on our past we can date our times by mentioning the types of vehicles which used our roads. We can fix the years when the words "covered wagon" or "Conestoga" or "horse and buggy" are brought up. Some day, perhaps, people will talk of the coming of the trucks, the period between World Wars I and II. American business for the first time since wagon days learned in those years to transport part of its rich burdens from one market to another without the help of the railroads.

The trucking business was a baby when the Yanks came home from France in 1919; today it has the muscles of a giant and enough pockets in its pants to hold over three billion dollars. It represents a swarm of seven million trucks at work for every recognizable industry in the country. These trucks, put bumper to bumper, would extend from California to New York, from New York across the Atlantic to England and halfway back again! They are unresting; their "land sailor" drivers cover a distance equal to fifty ten-ton load trips to the sun every year, hauling fifty billion-ton miles. Look in any store and there is scarcely an item that hasn't taken a truck ride. Trucks closed the era of the horse as man's bearer of burdens over our roads.

Back in 1899, when gentlemen wore mustaches and everybody rode bicycles, some enterprising stores abandoned horses and wagons for a few gasoline and electric delivery trucks on the cobbled streets of New York and Boston. A few years later the St. Louis *Post-Dispatch* stabled fifty horse-drawn newspaper wagons and delivered its papers in fourteen "motor delivery wagons." This was a rather daring experiment—and it proved that trucks were practical.

But such enterprise was, of course, confined to cities. The road-building boom was years away and the prospect of a system of good roads seemed a hope and a dream, if not downright impossible. With their weight and crude mechanisms, trucks simply could not traverse the mud and sinkholes of outlying roads. So by 1908 there were four thousand trucks in the United States, most of them engaged in city deliveries and the hauling of freight between railroad terminals.

One of these, a Sauer motor-truck appropriately named the "Pioneer Express," dared a long-distance run in 1911. Loaded with seven tons of freight, the truck plowed its way for fifteen hundred miles from Denver to Los Angeles. The run required sixty-six days, many of them spent by the four-man crew in clearing a path for the "Pioneer Express."

By 1916 there were 200,000 chugging, spluttering, mechanically uncertain trucks at work. Many people believed this was about as good as the trucking business could ever be; but the young giant had scarcely outgrown the cities. Beyond lay the vast inviting sweep of America to stretch and grow and flex its muscles in.

In 1917, when war began with Germany, the United States, in a transportation jam, assumed operation of the railroads and encouraged highway hauling by trucks. Thus truckers, forced out upon the roads, were shoved to opportunity. Army trucks, loaded with war goods for Europe, struggled mile by mile on bad roads from the West to eastern seaports. The drivers fought mud and detoured around holes, often cutting brush and trees from the roadsides. They forded streams, stopped at bridges which would not support their weight, and detoured again. They came to more mud. They cursed and swore they couldn't make it; but they kept on, somehow, and made it.

Bad as matters were, the truck was still better than the horse. Truck manufacturers soon saw the trend in their bookkeeping departments. The government wanted more, more, more trucks. Swamped with orders, the manufacturers sent their own trucks into the countryside to gather up materials with which to make more trucks for the armed services. The assembly lines stretched, and the truck became a fixture of American transportation, a familiar passerby on the roads.

When the soldiers returned from the war, they looked about for business opportunity. Each had his five-hundred-dollar service bonus and many looked upon the surging young trucking industry as a worthwhile field in which to invest and work. In business for themselves, they hauled whatever they could find. Loads were delivered from door to door and from city to city. "We can haul it," they said, "if it is loose at both ends."

Road-building progress, of course, was persistently with them. Right behind the road-building machinery were the trucking pioneers. They went anywhere the roads went, they paid no attention to the clock, and as business grew so did their fleet of trucks. By 1924 two million trucks were at work, by 1928 another million.

In trucking's early days it was a matter of grabbing a load here, taking it there, and wondering what tonnage could be found as a payload for the return trip. There was little system. The cargo-carrying planes in the years just after World War II passed through the same hit-or-miss, win-or-lose operation. But today cargo planes are settling down into the systematized routines of profitable operation long since practiced by truckers. Growing pains seem inescapable and the symptoms are similar where transportation is concerned.

Good roads for trucks, and trucks for whoever needs them have altered our way of living—and for the better. In the times when horses and wagons carried farm produce over almost impassable roads to railway shipping points, a farmer could hardly afford to live much more than ten miles from a rail line, just as it had been necessary for the early planters in Maryland, Virginia, and South Carolina to live near rivers. But with good roads farmers could live anywhere and make the most of rich good land, however remote. For this they could thank the truck. Transportation had become simply a matter of putting hogs or hens, pullets or pumpkins into the truck and striking out for market. And the long cattle drives over dusty western trails faded into cowboy history until there is left of them only the songs, the legends, and the nostalgia of old spurs hung for keepsakes on the wall. Cattle now ride to market or to the rail lines in trucks.

The effect on cities became apparent when trucks really got down to hard use, and there were solid roads for their wheels. Able to haul building materials cheaply and quickly for householders and stores, trucks turned much of the countryside into city suburbs. Thus, today, thousands of communities are dependent upon trucks and the good roads under their wheels for fuel, food, furniture, clothing—and the morning newspaper. Trucks have taken over almost entirely the handling of milk from farm to market and from dairy to consumer.

Just before America's entrance in World War II, trucks were hauling each year twenty-nine million tons of bituminous coal, seventy per cent of the nation's lumber, and 254,500 carloads of vegetables and fresh fruit. Daily life, more than we are likely to realize at first glance, is dependent upon trucks and good highways. It's all in the day's work to truckmen hauling prefabricated houses, yachts and cabin cruisers, airplanes, and the furniture for a ten-room house.

The truck driver we meet hunched over the pie and coffee has invented a language of his own. "A plow jockey buttoned her up, checked the bolognas and push-water, climbed into his housebroken cackle wagon, and drove off in training to be an Eskimo." Translated, the plow jockey is a cheap driver just off the farm; buttoning her up is tying on a truckload; bolognas are tires (undersized tires are rubber bands); push-water is gasoline; a cackle crate is a poultry truck and it is housebroken if it has no leaks; a driver is in training to be an Eskimo if he keeps his windows open.

The brisk crackle of the American truck driver's speech and the slouch of his walk into the millions of roadside eating places will be with us for many years. The airplane will make inroads upon his calling, but he will always be needed and will not disappear from our highways as did his forerunner with the long whip on the big wagons.

THE ROAD AHEAD

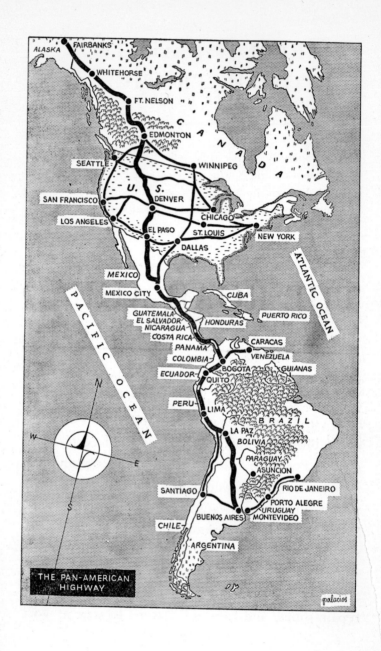

THE PAN-AMERICAN
HIGHWAY

palacios

22. FROM THE ARCTIC
TO THE TROPICS

I look hopefully to the time when the two continents of North America and South America will be united in physical fact through modern highways as they are today united by bonds of mutual friendship and good will.

Calvin Coolidge (1925)

When World War II thundered in the Pacific, Alaska was endangered, for the only way to get into that wide, deep land was by ship or by plane. After Pearl Harbor it was not certain that America could defend the shipping lanes of the Gulf of Alaska against enemy attack, and along with that uncertainty was the threat that the enemy might seize the Aleutians or get a foothold on the Alaskan coast, build a defendable airfield, and bomb Vancouver, Portland, Seattle, and even Chicago and San Francisco. Airfields were needed to repel such an invasion, and also a means of supplying the airfields. Strategically, it was desirable to place the fields and supply route behind the coastal ranges where they would not be exposed to sea-borne attack. "Bush" airfields, lacking adequate radio facilities, hangars, repair shops, and personnel, were located at Fort

St. John and Fort Nelson in British Columbia, and at Watson Lake and Whitehorse in Yukon Territory. To expand them involved transporting an enormous amount of equipment and building special barracks, kitchens, and sleeping quarters.

There was only one solution: the United States had to build a long-delayed overland road, a new northwest passage to Alaska to expand those flying fields and establish bases. That was the purpose in building the Alaskan Highway; but it would also become a truck route to provide Alaska with essential supplies should shipping become hazardous or impossible.

The construction of a highway connecting the United States and Canada with Alaska had been advocated for some years. In 1933 and again in 1940 congressional commissions submitted favorable reports on the proposal for a road through the great wilderness to Alaska; but nothing further was done until the disaster at Pearl Harbor made action imperative.

Pioneer road building always has been hard work, in whatever century; but never did road builders face such difficulties as on the Alaskan Highway. The road had to be slammed across fifteen hundred miles of wilderness country. The high, forbidding Canadian Rockies must be crossed; streams and rivers slashing through rolling country must be bridged somehow; stubborn trees rooted to the roadway must be cut down and their heavy stumps pulled up; miles of "bush," the second-growth aspen which follows forest fires, must be torn away; hundreds of miles of muskeg swamp, the bog of the North Country, must be crossed—and always dogging their steps were the mud and frost.

Everything moved fast once the decision to build a road was made. In March, 1942, by airplane, by dogsled, or on snowshoes, engineers of the Army and the Public Roads Administration explored the frozen mountain passes and followed the course of rivers, together locating the best route between control points. New-type aerial photographs, fitting together and giving depth somewhat as the old stereopticon slide pictures do, cut short the time for mapping out the route. The Canadian government dispensed with border duties, and sent men with dog teams off into the wilderness for reconnaisance.

Meanwhile, soldiers in U. S. Army camps were issued warm sleeping bags and parkas, and put on the march; freight trains were loaded with road machinery and quartermaster supplies, and rushed northward with priority over the tracks. Destination was Dawson Creek, the boom town in British Columbia where the railroad tracks ended and the highway was to begin. The Army had undertaken, in one short construction season between early spring thaw and autumn freeze, to cut through a pioneer road, establish camps, and bring in equipment. Brig. Gen. William M. Hoge commanded the building of the northern stretch of road from his headquarters at Whitehorse. Working up from the south were soldiers under Col. J. A. (Patsy) O'Connor.

Soon after midnight on March 9 the first troops piled off the train into a dark barren country and twenty-five degrees below-zero cold. They slept on the frozen ground for a few hours, and went to work the next morning. The soldiers, white and colored, who slashed, tugged, sweated, and built the pioneer road were mostly untrained for their hard job. They had been lawyers, clerks, messengers, farmers, "grease monkeys," musicians, students, truck drivers —a cross-section of workers, as throughout the Army.

Every kind of road-building machinery was put to work on the Alaskan Highway: bulldozers, trucks, power shovels, graders, snow plows, and the big Caterpillar tractors nicknamed simply "cats." To the contractors' construction equipment the government added machinery left over from road-building operations of the Civilian Conservation Corps. Altogether there were about five thousand pieces of machinery, some of it held together by welding torches and the roadside patching done by portable repair shops. Out in the wilderness were Public Roads surveying parties, blazing trees, giving the line to the Army.

From Dawson Creek the highway leads forty-nine miles to Fort St. John, the jumping-off place, thence 250 miles north to Fort Nelson. Here the road swings northwesterly for more than six hundred miles by Watson Lake and on to Whitehorse in the Yukon. From this frontier town the road leads through Alaska's Tanana Crossing, Big Delta, and on to the terminal, Fairbanks.

A passable dirt road led from Dawson Creek the few miles to Fort St. John. There the Army boys put up the first road sign on the Alaskan Highway: an arrow pointing confidently north, reading "Fairbanks, 1,459." The soldier road builders were welcomed at the jumping-off place. In a vacant store the women of the town organized a coffee-and-doughnut bar and contributed a piano.

At Dawson Creek, at the very outset, the road builders faced a desperate problem: they had to move troops, huge machinery, and tons of supplies to Fort Nelson, the engineers' camp about three hundred miles north. Only a winter trail connected the two places, and when the spring thaw came the trail was turned into an impassable bog. Also, five rivers, including the Peace and Sikanni Chief, now quietly frozen, must be passed while their hard icy surface would still support the heavy trucks. Canadian trappers expected the thaw around April 1.

The soldiers of the 35th Engineer Regiment, commanded by Col. Robert D. Ingalls, picked for this first hard task, had only a few weeks for its completion and they didn't waste any time. Day and night, trucks lumbered back and forth over the tundra, each with one man driving, another sleeping. Rolling over the frozen river into Fort Nelson, they dumped their loads and immediately turned back to Dawson Creek for another load. Then the first thaw came, before the job was completed. The soldiers threw heavy planks and sawdust on their roadway across Peace River, but in desperation they saw the river breaking up under them. Suddenly, and just then, a terrible freeze came. The river held, and the soldiers rushed across. All of the men, machinery, and nine hundred tons of supplies reached Fort Nelson by April 5.

Ahead was the job of building a pioneer road; but the first gamble with time and weather had been won. One Army truck driver looked back, shook his fist at the wild Peace River, and laughed at it: "Go ahead, old man, and bust wide open of you want to. We've got you licked!"

The snow began to melt and rain came. It rained for days and the soft soil became a bogging muck. Big "cats" sank, sometimes as deep as the drivers' seats, were pulled out, and clawed on again. Gradually, the soldiers pushed the forest back from the roadway. The rain left soft, spongy, orange-black muskeg covering deep mudpits, and over these the road builders simply piled aspen, spruce, and pine logs to make a corduroy road surface as their ancestors had done more than 150 years earlier. Overhead was the drone of Army photo planes. Road locaters, mapping the route from these aerial pictures, avoided muskeg for all but fifteen miles or so. Frequently the surveyors were only thirty miles ahead of the men cutting down trees and bush.

Quartermaster supplies and equipment, pontoon battalions, combat engineers, and medical units were strung through the bush country, served by trucks slogging over the new road. Before this feverish American activity only Indians and scarlet-coated Canadian Mounties had been in that wilderness country. The men, eating Army field rations and sleeping in pup tents, worked in ten-hour shifts seven days a week. As the days grew warmer mosquitos came to harass them. Sometimes the insects were so thick the soldiers had to raise their voices to be heard above the constant hum. But the pioneer road was pushed northward, toward Watson Lake just over the Yukon border. Following the soldiers were the men of the Public Roads Administration, widening, grading, and smoothing the road.

Simultaneously the northern section of the highway was stretching out from headquarters at Whitehorse, the town of 330 prewar population that had been born in the Klondike days. One of the old steamers that had carried the sourdoughs from Whitehorse to Alaska was still at the town, pulled up on shore. Large steamers still go from the town, down the Lewes and Yukon, to interior Alaska. It was here that Robert W. Service had clerked in a bank (the same bank at which American soldiers now cashed their Army checks); and from Whitehorse, Rex Beach and Jack London had located their stories of the Yukon in the gold rush days.

The soldiers obtained special permission from the Yukon government to hunt, and were able to supplement their Army food with moose and bear steak, lake trout, venison, spruce partridge, and grouse. At night they trudged the muddy streets, passing malemute dog teams tied up, or stray malemutes roaming the town, and they packed the frontier Whitehorse Inn, played mouth organs and sang with careful barbershop harmony.

The same procedure was followed in this section as at Fort St. John in British Columbia; bases and camps were set up in March to take advantage of the frozen rivers. The days were nearly twenty-four hours long, but the "land of the midnight sun" posed quite unromantic road-building problems. The

"cat" drivers, tearing away moss, came upon ice—
and the sun melted away their roadbed. They put
the moss back and made a corduroy road over the
frozen ground. During the next summer civilian
workers using bulldozers pushed aside the muskeg
and filled in the roadbed with firm soil.

Northwest from Whitehorse the Alaskan Highway
followed for a while a trail left by the gold rushers
of '98; but after that again there was only untouched
wilderness into Alaska.

When the road reached Fairbanks, the Army's
job was about completed, but the Alaskan Highway
was still a pioneer or "tote" road, with steep grades
and sharp curves. Its surface was not all-weather; the
road had led wherever a bulldozer could force its
way in the shortest time, and the numerous bridges
were mostly trestles built from native lumber. The
announcement of its "completion" in November,
1942, was a strategic move for purposes of wartime
propaganda, for the road was built largely during the
1943 construction season by contractors' forces from
the United States and Canada. But the tremendous
undertaking could not have been completed so
quickly without the Army-built pioneer road.

Working from camps on an average more than two
thousand miles from home, the eighty-one contractors faced the problem of bringing in additional
heavy road-building machinery—six thousand units

were used altogether—and the transportation of fifteen thousand civilian workers and all the equipment for their feeding and housing. The Public Health Service organized a fine medical and hospital service, and kept health conditions at a high level through inspections of camp sanitation and water supplies.

Equipped with arctic clothing, the men at most camps, working in two shifts of eleven hours each, kept their machines going twenty-two hours a day. Bridges had to be built over many large rivers—the Hyland, Coal, Liard, Muskwa, Sikanni Chief, Peace, and Kiskatinaw, and over glacial streams such as the Johnson, Tanana, Donjek, and Duke Rivers. Repair shops were kept open day and night, for during the winter months when temperatures dropped to forty or fifty degrees below zero, the heavy machinery frequently broke down, particularly when working in muskeg and beds of great boulders. Even under light loads, drive shafts snapped and frozen grease put gears out of operation.

In October the military highway was completed. Access roads connected it with the airports, and since the roadway followed the general air route, it was a guide to pilots in bad flying weather. Never in history had such a long stretch of road been built so quickly, and under such difficulties.

Today the Alaskan Highway has an all-weather surface, mostly graveled. Of course, there are not yet the fine accommodations for tourists—hotels, resorts, garages—that will come later. Most of the travel on the highway today is by job-seekers heading for Alaska. There are some tourists, "pleased with themselves at having accomplished the last really big motoring adventure on this continent."

F. C. Durkin, making the first official inspection trip for the American Automobile Association, said: "I have enjoyed this trip to Alaska. It has been a novel experience. . . . I would say that we encountered a minimum of difficulty and perhaps made the trip as easily as it has ever been made, both in operating the car and finding accommodations. We had bed rolls or sleeping bags along and only used them once in a barracks building converted to a tourist cabin affair, where we thought the sleeping bags were cleaner than the bedding. It was never necessary to use the extra gas we carried in the trunk."

Alaskans are somewhat amused at stateside people who prefer summer driving. They themselves would just as soon strike "outside" when the road has a smooth covering of snow, and worries with dust or mosquitos do not present themselves. The A.A.A. report speaks for them: "It is not necessary to bring trunks of parkas and heavy woolen clothes to Alaska in the summer. People arriving on some of the packaged tours are still making their debuts on the docks, airfields, and in railroad stations looking like candidates for Admiral Byrd's next polar jaunt. The summer is just like it is in nearly any part of the northern United States."

The vast undeveloped area pierced by the Alaskan Highway is rich in natural resources—gold, silver, lead, copper, coal. Millions of waterfowl nest in the lonesome Rocky Mountain country, and the forests abound with game and good pulpwood for paper.

On their journey toward the Arctic, travelers over the new road will see the high Canadian Rockies; they will pass great rivers and hundreds of lakes, muskeg swamps, and endless spruce forests. Riding over permanently frozen ground, they may see an occasional trapper's cabin, or Indians to whom English is a strange language. If they drive in midsummer, before the Arctic winter moves over the Yukon, the weather will be cool and the days bright and sunny. Twilight will last through most of the night, and many travelers will be treated to a front-seat view of the spectacular northern lights.

The highway, beginning as an undertaking against a common enemy of the United States and Canada, is now a link in the good friendship between the latter countries. In April, 1946, under the terms of an agreement, the Canadian section of the road was turned over to Canada.

The Alaskan Highway will become a trade route, as are all commercial roads; and it will become a much-traveled road for vacationing tourists. Travel-loving Americans, as you might expect, had their eyes on the Alaskan Highway before the Army had finished cutting a pioneer road out of the wilderness.

For years people have been talking about a hemispheric system of highways—of good roads south of the Rio Grande, connecting all of the South American countries with Central America, Mexico, the United States, and Canada. Today that dream—the Pan-American Highway System—is progressing toward reality.

Back in 1929 the Pan-American Highway Congress, meeting at Rio de Janeiro, worked out a general plan for the road system, and engineers from North and Central America joined forces, working on plans for the part of the road from the United States–Mexican border to Panama called the Inter-American Highway. The countries agreed to have the road meet at the various borders, and each started its own road-building program.

At the time of Pearl Harbor, in December, 1941, South America had three thousand miles of paved road and five thousand miles of all-weather road. The Inter-American Highway from Laredo, Texas, to Panama had over a thousand miles of paved road and six hundred miles of all-weather road. This mileage was not continuous, however, and with the coming of the war the incomplete road from the United States to the Panama Canal assumed real importance as a possible military highway. Congress began making appropriations to close the gaps, and at once the highway departments of each country, with the cooperation of the Public Roads Administration of the U.S.A., pushed ahead on the hard road-building job. Mexico, handling its own surveying, engineering, and road construction problems, was the exception.

By the following July, United States Army engineers were hacking through the mountains and jungles of Central America. The road builders were fine heroes to the inhabitants of the villages through which the highway passed. These people, with no concern over the military or potential peacetime uses of the long highway, thought only of its importance to their own village. They prepared their best food for the road builders, and organized special fiestas in their honor.

The engineers, here as in Alaska, faced terrible difficulties. They had to push through jungles, climb high mountains, and frequently uproot giant trees, including oaks 125 feet high and twenty-five feet around. Often it took as many pounds of dynamite as a tree was tall to uproot it.

Today the highway is still incomplete. Only a few gaps remain, however, and when these are closed a new motoring adventure—this time to the tropics—

Grading machines cutting and leveling the roadbed of the Atlantic Highway through heavy forest on the Isthmus of Panama.

Section of the Alaskan Highway, near the border. The hoar frost on the trees makes this a scene of fairyland beauty.

View of road network around the Lincoln Memorial, Washington, D. C., showing approach to Memorial Bridge across the Potomac River.

Grade separation on Merritt Parkway in Connecticut. This four-lane express highway conforms to standards recommended for heavily traveled sections of the National Interstate Highway System.

Lake Shore Drive, a six-lane expressway along the lake front, carries large volumes of traffic to and from downtown Chicago.

Aerial view of traffic interchange and overpass on U. S. 4, near Gordon's Corner, New Jersey. This type of interchange is being introduced in highway construction throughout the country.

Design for Grant Circle underpass on the Cross-Bronx Expressway, N. Y.

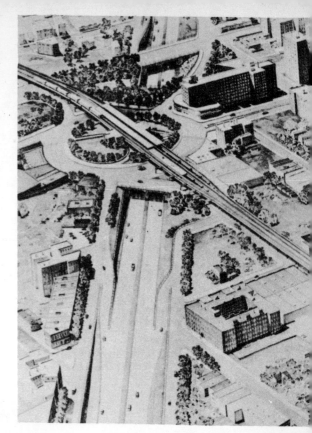

Traffic interchange plan for the Congress Street Expressway, Chicago.

will beckon American travelers. The road follows high mountains thousands of feet above the sea, dips into dense tropical jungles, and brings together old and new—primitive oxcarts and modern trucks and automobiles. Longer than the east-west route from New York to San Francisco, the highway extends 3,356 miles to the Canal from Mexico's Nuevo Laredo, opposite Laredo, Texas.

In Mexico vacationing Americans will see the pyramids of Quetzalcoatl, where the Aztecs offered human sacrifices; the aqueduct built by the Spaniards three hundred years ago at Los Remedios, and Popocatepetl, the famous snow-capped volcano. In the lower and warmer regions are sub-tropical valleys laced with orange groves and sugar and banana plantations. Crossing the Tropic of Cancer below Cuidad Victoria the road enters dense jungle country where brightly colored birds scream from the trees and orchids grow wild. Mexicans have named the section of their road leading from Mexico City to Guatemala the "Christopher Columbus Highway." Guatemalans, jumping about five hundred years of history, named their road the "Franklin D. Roosevelt Highway."

The "F.D.R." road passes over a 200-foot-long arch bridge built by Spanish slaves in 1592. From low tropical jungle country the road rises, in forty miles, to a height of seven thousand feet. Always in

sight of the road, as it passes through jungle, mountains, and ancient Indian villages, are Guatemala's
volcanoes.

El Salvador's 191 miles of road lead through rolling hills past Lake Coatepeque, at the foot of an
extinct volcano, and on through hills and rich valleys, crossing the Lempa River over Cuscatlan
Bridge, the longest suspension bridge in Central
America. Honduras' ninety-five-mile stretch of the
highway offers a fine scenic view of the Bay of
Fonseca. The long road in Nicaragua and Costa Rica
—over six hundred miles combined—passes coffee
and banana plantations, and more extinct volcanoes.
At one point in Costa Rica it climbs straight up the
continental divide, a rise of six thousand feet in
twenty miles. The traveler is then eleven thousand
feet high, moving along the crest of the Talamanca
range. On a clear day he can see the Atlantic
Ocean fifty miles away and the Pacific Ocean thirty
miles away.

The road passes long stretches of beautiful tropical
beaches in Panama, and from Panama City leads to
the ruins of the former capital, Old Panama, which
the ruthless pirate Henry Morgan destroyed in
1671. Fifty miles beyond, the road ends.

Already many tourists have made the journey for
such distances as the road permits; soon many others
will follow as the project nears completion, and the

money they will spend will have an economic importance in each country, as in Mexico today. But the real value of the Inter-American Highway will be in the opportunities for trade it offers. The United States will be able to obtain products which must now be imported from the Far East—vegetable oils, mahogany, quinine, cinnamon, tea, rice, and rubber; Costa Rica and Guatemala can export their fine coffee, honey, and citrus fruits, their rare balsam and rosewood. In return, as trade increases, "Made in the U.S.A." stoves, refrigerators, bathtubs, and farm machinery will find a new market.

Nor will the trade advantage of the road be wholly in the export and import line. Citizens of Nicaragua and Costa Rica, for instance, now find it cheaper to import rice from the Orient than to haul their own good rice over the high mountains in their countries. And, in Guatemala, with eighteen million acres of fine forests, pine from Oregon is imported; it is cheaper than hauling by oxcart from the interior. This is reminiscent of America's transportation difficulties in the past, when farmers floated their goods thousands of miles to New Orleans, rather than send them by pack horse or Conestoga wagon over the Allegheny Mountains.

23. TODAY'S HIGHWAYS

The use of the principal highways is so extensive that people pay for adequate roads whether they have them or not, and they pay more if they have them than if they have not.

Thomas H. MacDonald
Commissioner of Public Roads

Many miles of modern roads, beginning as Indian trails and buffalo traces, have seen the whole sweep of America on the move: the first few lonely men on horseback, the strong patient men in sturdy oxcarts and trader wagons, the men and women who passed in covered wagons and stage-coaches, and the hardy citizens, also pioneers in their way, who plowed through mud and dust in early rickety automobiles and trucks.

There are three million miles of rural highways in the United States. About half of them are all-weather surfaced. Gravel, soil, or low-cost bituminous surfacing cover 1,300,000 miles; high-type Portland cement concrete covers 200,000 miles. There are also 300,000 miles of city streets, many miles of which, of course, were once country roads until cities grew up around them.

The roads are all numbered, and each number has its meaning. In the U. S. Highway system, east-west roads are marked by even numbers. Of these, the lower numbers indicate roads in the northern part of the country. Major east-west routes are multiples of 10 from 10 to 90. Other U. S. Highways with even two-digit numbers are still east-west roads, though not as important generally.

Odd U. S. Highway numbers mark north-south roads, with the lower numbers indicating roads in the eastern part of the country. The most important of these north-south roads are marked with two-digit numbers ending in 1 or 5 (with one exception, U. S. 101 which runs the whole length of the Pacific Coast).

Sometimes a main route has alternate courses, each passing through an important city. Then the route number stays the same, but is marked: U. S. 40 N (orth) or U.S. 40 S (outh).

Out in the country the markers are about three and one-half feet above the ground, so that head-lights may pick them up easily. When the through-route enters a city the markers are raised to seven feet so they may be seen above cars parked on the streets.

Some states also number those state roads which are a part of the U. S. Highway system. The black-and-white U. S. Highway shield is the same all over the country, but state signs, usually on the same standard, vary. South Dakota has an Indian head; Texas, a star; Nebraska, a covered wagon, and Ohio an outline map of the state.

Except for California's Route 101, all three-digit roads have a special reason for their numbers. The two right-hand numbers are always the main route to which the road is an alternate course or tributary. Route 211, for example, is a feeder road for Route 11. The first numeral means something, too. The "2" means that Route 211 is the second feeder road counting from the north of Route 11. In the same way, Route 240 is the second feeder from the east of Route 40. The principal "named"* highways of earlier days now carry various highway numbers.

The story is told of an elderly woman from Boston's Beacon Hill who once discovered by a roadside an abandoned, moss-grown marker which she thought was a gravestone. She traced out the faint "1 M. FROM BOSTON," and with the usual pride in her city, read aloud: "I'm from Boston. How simple! How sufficient!" Road experts like to tell this story to show that simplicity and sufficiency are all that is needed on any sign, be it roadside or grave. Over a period of years, with all of the forty-eight states co-operating, the United States has developed a

*See Appendix.

standard and simple system of traffic signs, markings, and signals, familiar to all motorists.

Over the three million miles of roads each year automobiles and trucks are driven some 395 billion vehicle miles. More than half of all the tonnage transported in the United States is hauled over the highways. Each year more than fifteen and one-half billion dollars is spent on the operation of cars, trucks, and buses. Nearly everything we eat and wear and use has been out on the road somewhere in getting to us.

Keeping highways in operation is a steady job for the 327,000 people who are employed in construction and maintenance alone. Americans spend a lot of money on their roads, for good roads cost money —one mile of concrete highway costs fifty thousand dollars or more to build. In 1950, nearly two billion dollars was allotted for highway construction, and another billion and a half for highway maintenance.

Still, the roads are not good enough. Many are obsolete, and nearly all suffer from the creaking infirmities of a too-active old age. On some roads the surface is obsolete, on many others repairs are long overdue; and roads today are too narrow, too crooked, and too rambling. Seldom are cities connected by the most direct route. Today, as always in the past, vehicles are far ahead of roads.

Long stretches out in the country are good enough to permit an average speed of forty-seven miles per hour. But when roads approach cities it is easy to see that they have long been out of date. Motorists who have inched and crawled through endless miles of slow-moving cars, trying to enter or leave a city, know how inadequate our roads are. "Something ought to be done about this road," they grumble. The expression—a typically American complaint— is frequently and justifiably heard on our highways. George Washington probably could have gone through parts of Baltimore by stagecoach or on horseback making much better time than a car-driving traveler today.

There are some expressways scattered across the continent which anticipate the much-discussed "highway of tomorrow." San Francisco has a fine system of approaches to the Golden Gate Bridge and its Bay Bridge. Los Angeles has the Cahuenga Pass Freeway, and the Arroyo Seco Parkway, linking that city with Pasadena. New York is served by the Pulaski Skyway, and a splendid 400-mile network of expressways. Chicago's Outer Drive is a real achievement in highway planning.

Pennsylvania today, as in the past, is one of the leaders in road building. With its hundred-mile long toll road called the Pennsylvania Turnpike, the state has finally conquered its ancient enemy to transportation, the Alleghenies, for the Turnpike leads through ventilated tunnels which cut right through the mountains. The entire length can be driven without a single stop for a traffic light, or even a shift of gear. Connecticut's Merritt Parkway, also a toll road, offers comparable speed and safety.

But these roads are exceptional. The thought of fifty million automobiles and trucks out on our "modern" highways within a few years is an appalling one to road specialists. Nearly one-third of our main state highways need improvement of some kind; fourteen thousand miles of two-lane highways serve four-lane traffic. Thirty thousand bridges need rebuilding and widening.

Several hundred thousand miles of county and local roads are badly in need of grading, draining, and surfacing—and these are important farm-to-market roads. Nearly half of America's farms are still on dirt roads. We still have roads classed as "primitive"—861,000 miles of them—roads that are as bad now as they were during the horse and buggy era.

World War II held back the road-building job at least five years, for work was limited to the construction and improvement of access roads leading to military bases and to plants manufacturing munitions and war goods. During the war our highways were a real line of national defense. They were crowded with civilian workers in war plants, with trucks hauling vital parts and raw materials for the assembly line. Because America had a fine highway system it was possible to swing rapidly into the tremendous war production job; but the war made Americans realize more than ever how dependent we are on our highways, and how inadequate they are for modern needs, whether in peace or war.

Back in the heyday of the road-building boom, during the late twenties and early thirties, the chief goal was to "get the farmer out of the mud"—and that back-breaking task was just about accomplished. But serious mistakes in planning were made—mistakes resulting in traffic congestion today. The planners did not foresee that in a few short years nearly every family would own a car; that thousands of buses would be on the roads, and that trucks would swing so urgently into the transportation picture. Traffic soon jammed those "modern" roads and made many of them obsolete. During the fifteen years before World War II an average of 31,000 to 33,000 people were killed in traffic accidents each year, and more than a million were injured. Property damage resulting from highway accidents ran into millions of dollars.

When congestion in cities began to be a problem, people started thinking about transcontinental highways that would by-pass cities entirely. "We are out of the mud," they said, "now let's get out of this bumper-to-bumper muddle." Everybody demanded road improvement. Cities complained that while their streets were overcrowded, money was being spent on country roads; the farm bloc meanwhile asked for further road appropriations.

In 1936 the Public Roads Administration, cooperating with the state highway departments, began a highway planning study, the most comprehensive ever undertaken. Its purpose was to find out where road money came from and where it went; how much city people paid toward roads, and how much country people paid; how many people traveled over each road, and for what purpose; and, of course, the actual condition of each road and its suitability for future traffic. Thousands of motorists all over the country, all through the year and in all kinds of weather, were stopped and asked where they came from and where they were going. Traffic was charted on all rural roads.

As a result of the survey it was found that we cannot get out of the traffic muddle by by-passing cities, for people want to get into them. The most urgent highway need is not for super transcontinental routes, but for the elimination of bottlenecks at cities.

Most of us, the survey showed, drive less than thirty miles one way when we take the car out.

When we leave city limits, two-thirds of the time we travel less than ten miles. We are on the move all the time, but only for short distances, although many of us take a couple of long trips each year.

Another rather startling fact was brought out by the survey: about forty thousand miles of road—only 1.3 per cent of the total mileage—carry 20 per cent of our traffic. Under a plan recommended by the Public Roads Administration, these forty thousand miles (called the National Interstate Highway System) will become the expressways of the future.

Today our roads are at a turning point; but at least we know now what is needed and what we have to do. The federal government has appropriated vast sums for road building, and long-range planning gives some assurance that when we do have these expressways, they will not become obsolete before they wear out.

24. THE ROAD AHEAD

Two hundred miles an hour would revolutionize the business and social world. Old lines would be turned upside down and all present systems relegated to history. Let it come!

Munsey's Magazine (1900)

Two thousand years ago the Romans built good strong roads, the lifeline of their empire. These lasted through many centuries, and some of them are still in use. The roads we are planning and building in the United States today are far better than any the Romans ever built—and should last as long. We cannot say how long they will be adequate, because we cannot anticipate the vehicle of the distant future. But we do know that the system of roads now mostly in the blueprint stage will be far superior to any highways the world has ever seen, and they will last as long as we can see into the future now. Perhaps as many as ten, fifteen, or even twenty years will pass before we actually have under our wheels all the completed mileage planned for our expressways and other roads. Forty thousand miles of expressways, or freeways, will connect all of our cities and larger towns. These are the "Interregional

Highways" which compose the National System of Interstate Highways.

Let's look ahead into these years: out in the country, the roads in this system resemble the modern Pennsylvania Turnpike and Connecticut's Merritt Parkway, except for stretches through desert country and little-populated areas where traffic does not justify expressway treatment. Otherwise, there is no cross-traffic (overhead bridges take care of that); no stop lights, dangerous curves, or steep climbs harass motorists and truck drivers. The horror of head-on collisions is a memory, for expressways have divided lanes. Traffic moves in one direction only on each lane, at a smooth sixty, seventy, or seventy-five miles an hour.

The expressways do not stop at the front doors of cities and towns, as roads used to. They follow cloverleaf patterns, similar to those on the road approaching the Pentagon Building near Washington D. C., built during World War II. The new kind of city street, now a highway through the city, continues right into and through the business centers, and even then there are no traffic lights or pedestrians. Ramps spaced every few blocks enable motorists to get on or off the expressway, and right into the heart of the city—or quickly away from it. Through some cities the expressway rises above the ground; in others it lies below the city streets.

Imagine the time that is saved, compared to the slow crawl through cities of the 1940's. Every day, 224 years of driving time is saved, compared to the driving time of the past. With traffic hazards eliminated, thousands of lives are saved each year. The old highway mortality figures appall citizens of the future, who take expressways for granted.

For many years the whole trend of industry has been toward centralization. People were attracted to towns and big cities, where they could find better jobs and better schools for their children, and music, libraries, theatres, and recreation for themselves. People usually said, "This is the road *to* San Francisco" or "*to* New York" or "*to* Dallas" or "*to* New Orleans"; seldom was a road described as being *from* a city.

We can see the beginning of future changes right now, the changes that may lead us to think of highways as being from, as well as to, the cities. People can live anywhere, and with all the comforts of city dwelling, since fuel, food, and everything necessary to living can be brought to them by truck over highways. Automobiles can take them back and forth to work, school buses can take their children to and from good schools. Factories built on any highway in the United States are now connected with every other factory, because of highway transportation. Thus industries are able to spread their assembly lines, and decentralize. Many already have done this. In this atomic age it seems a good thing to do, for industrial as well as military reasons. When the country is connected by fast expressways it is probable that the outward trend will be accelerated.

On our roads of the future, all over the United States, main highways connect with the expressways. These are wider, straighter, and in better condition than they used to be. So are feeder roads leading into the main roads from farms. The old frontiers on the North American continent are gone—motorists may drive in comfort and safety from any place in the United States north to Alaska, and see the midnight sun of the Arctic Circle; or south to the Panama Canal and see the Southern Cross of tropical night skies.

APPENDIX

ROUTES OF PRINCIPAL NAMED HIGHWAYS IN THE UNITED STATES

ATLANTIC HIGHWAY—Ft. Kent, Me., Van Buren, Houlton, Calais, Ellsworth, Bangor, Belfast, Rockland, Bath, Portland, Kittery, Me.; Portsmouth, N. H.; Newburyport, Mass., Salem, Boston, Mass.; Providence, R. I., Westerly, R. I.; New London, Conn., New Haven, Bridgeport, Conn.; New York, N. Y.; Jersey City, N. J., Newark, Trenton, N. J. Philadelphia Pa.; Wilmington, Del.; Baltimore, Md.; Washington, D. C.; Alexandria, Va., Fredericksburg, Richmond, Petersburg, Va.; Henderson, N. C., Raleigh, Southern Pines, Rockingham, N. C.; Cheraw, S. C., Columbia, S. C.; Augusta, Ga., Savannah, Brunswick, Ga.; Jacksonville, Fla., St. Augustine, Daytona Beach, Ft. Pierce, West Palm Beach, Miami, Fla.

DIXIE HIGHWAY (Western Division)—Sault Ste. Marie, Mich., Mackinaw City, Traverse City, Muskegon, St. Joseph, Mich.; South Bend, Ind., Indianapolis, New Albany, Ind.; Louisville, Ky., Bowling

Green, Ky.; Nashville, Tenn., Chattanooga, Tenn.; Atlanta, Ga., Macon, Waycross, Ga.; Jacksonville, Fla. Branch: Chicago, Ill., Danville, Ill.; Indianapolis, Ind. Branch: Macon, Ga., Americus, Thomasville, Ga; Tallahassee, Fla., Gainesville, Orlando, Indian River City, Punta Gorda, Marco, Miami, Fla.

LEE HIGHWAY—New York, N. Y.; Newark, N. J.; Trenton, N. J.; Philadelphia, Pa.; Baltimore, Md.; Washington, D. C.; New Market, Va., Staunton, Lexington, Roanoke, Va., Bristol, Va.—Tenn.; Knoxville, Tenn., Chattanooga, Tenn.; Huntsville, Ala., Florence, Ala.; Corinth, Miss.; Memphis, Tenn.; Little Rock, Ark., Hot Springs, DeQueen, Ark.; Durant, Okla., Ardmore, Frederick, Okla.; Vernon, Tex., Plainview, Tex.; Clovis, N. M., Roswell, N. M.; El Paso, Tex.; Lordsburg, N. M.; Globe, Ariz., Phoenix, Yuma, Ariz; San Diego, Calif., Los Angeles, Santa Barbara, San Luis Obispo, Paso Robles, San Jose, San Francisco, Calif.

LINCOLN HIGHWAY—New York, N. Y.; Newark, N. J., Trenton, N. J.; Philadelphia, Pa., Lancaster, York, Gettysburg, Bedford, Pittsburgh, Pa.; East Liverpool, Ohio, Canton, Delphos, Ohio; Fort Wayne, Ind., Valparaiso, Ind.; Joliet, Ill., Geneva, Sterling, Ill.; Clinton, Ia., Cedar Rapids, Marshalltown, Denison, Council Bluffs, Ia.; Omaha, Neb., Columbus,

Kearney, Big Spring, Neb.; Cheyenne, Wyo., Rawlins, Rock Springs, Wyo.; Salt Lake City, Utah; Ely, Nev., Reno, Nev.; Sacramento, Calif., Oakland, San Francisco, Calif. Branch: Fallon, Nev., Carson City, Nev.; Placerville, Calif., Sacramento, Calif.

MERIDIAN HIGHWAY—Winnipeg, Man., Letellier, Man.; Grand Forks, N. D., Fargo, N. D.; Watertown, S. D., Yankton, S. D.; Columbus, Neb.; Salina, Kan., Wichita, Kan.; Enid, Okla., Chickasha, Comanche, Okla.; Ft. Worth, Tex., Waco, Austin, San Antonio, Laredo, Tex.; Monterrey, Mex., Mexico City, Mex. Branch: Waco, Tex., to Houston, Tex.

NATIONAL OLD TRAILS ROAD—Baltimore, Md.; Washington, D. C.; Frederick, Md., Hagerstown, Cumberland, Md.; Washington, Pa.; Wheeling, W. Va.; Zanesville, Ohio, Columbus, Dayton, Ohio; Indianapolis, Ind., Terre Haute, Ind.; Vandalia, Ill., East St. Louis, Ill.; St. Louis, Mo., Kansas City, Mo.; Council Grove, Kans., McPherson, Dodge City, Kan.; La Junta, Colo., Trinidad, Colo.; Raton, N. M., Santa Fe, Socorro, N. M.; St. Johns, Ariz., Holbrook, Williams, Kingman, Ariz.; Needles, Calif., Barstow, San Bernardino, Pasadena, Los Angeles, Calif.

OLD SPANISH TRAIL—Jacksonville, Fla., Tallahassee, Pensacola, Fla.; Mobile, Ala.; New Orleans, La.;

Beaumont, Tex., Houston, San Antonio, Sonora, Van Horn, El Paso, Tex.; Lordsburg, N. M.; Tucson, Ariz., Phoenix, Yuma, Ariz.; San Diego, Calif. Branch: San Antonio to Del Rio, and Van Horn, Tex.

PACIFIC HIGHWAY—Vancouver, B. C.; Blaine, Wash., Seattle, Tacoma, Olympia, Vancouver, Wash.; Portland, Ore., Salem, Eugene, Medford, Ore.; Dunsmuir, Calif., Red Bluff, Williams, Oakland, San Francisco, San Jose, Paso Robles, San Luis Obispo, Santa Barbara, Los Angeles, San Diego, Calif.

PIKES PEAK OCEAN-TO-OCEAN HIGHWAY—New York, N. Y.; Trenton, N. J.; Philadelphia, Pa., Harrisburg, Hollidaysburg, Blairsville, Washington, Pa.; Coshocton, Ohio, Bellefontaine, Ohio; Anderson, Ind.; Danville, Ill., Decatur, Springfield, Ill.; Hannibal, Mo., Chillicothe, St. Joseph, Mo.; Marysville, Kan., Colby, Kan.; Limon, Colo., Colorado Springs, Grand Junction, Colo.; Price, Utah, Beaver, St. George, Utah; Las Vegas, Nev.; Barstow, Calif.; San Bernardino, Pasadena, Los Angeles, Calif.

YELLOW TRAIL—Boston, Mass., Worcester, Springfield, Pittsfield, Mass.; Albany, N. Y., Schenectady, Utica, Syracuse, Auburn, Buffalo, N. Y.; Erie, Pa.;

Ashtabula, Ohio, Cleveland, Sandusky, Toledo, Bryan, Ohio; Ft. Wayne, Ind., Valparaiso, Gary, Ind.; Chicago, Ill., Waukegan, Ill.; Kenosha, Wis.; Milwaukee, Oshkosh, Stevens Point, Marshfield, Eau Claire, Wis.; St. Paul, Minn., Minneapolis, Ortonville, Minn.; Aberdeen, S. D., Mobridge, Lemmon, S. D.; Marmarth, N. D.; Fallon, Mont., Miles City, Billings, Livingston, Yellowstone National Park, Butte, Missoula, Mont.; Wallace, Idaho; Spokane, Wash., Walla Walla, Yakima, Cle Elum, Seattle, Wash.

Compiled by the American Automobile Association